THE
KINDNESS
METHOD

CHANGING HABITS
FOR GOOD

SHAHROO IZADI

bluebird
books for life

First published 2018 by Bluebird
an imprint of Pan Macmillan
20 New Wharf Road, London N1 9RR
Associated companies throughout the world
www.panmacmillan.com

ISBN 978-1-5098-8182-6

Copyright © Shahroo Izadi 2018

9 8 7 6 5 4 3 2 1

A CIP catalogue record for this book is available from the British Library.

Designed and typeset by Andrew Barron @ Thextension

Printed and bound by CPI Group (UK) Ltd, Croydon, CR0 4YY

The advice in this book is not intended to replace medical help from a
qualified doctor.

Visit www.panmacmillan.com to read more about all our books
and to buy them. You will also find features, author interviews and
news of any author events, and you can sign up for e-newsletters
so that you're always first to hear about our new releases.

To the young women at Amy's Place

CONTENTS

FOREWORD

—

In the summer of 2016, over the course of six coffees, Shahroo Izadi changed my life.

At the time I was writing a series of articles for *The Pool*, investigating my relationship with wine. I'd contacted her to see if she could not only help shape the feature, but help me figure out what was going on: I was in the pub, *again*, on a Tuesday night, *again*, with nothing inside me except a bottle of wine and a packet of crisps, *again*. Wine was my response to stress, celebration, relaxation, a Monday night, a Sunday afternoon. It didn't matter. I always wanted a drink.

The change that Shahroo brought to my life, however, wasn't one of dramatic reinvention which, when we think of narratives around dealing with alcohol problems, or indeed breaking any habit, is often how the story goes. Because that wasn't really the intention. I didn't want to stop drinking or even believe I needed too.

Shahroo Izadi changed my life because she allowed me to have a conversation with myself I never otherwise would have.

And that's Shahroo's magic. It's as if she leads you to a back door in your own head, a secret one away from all the anxieties and insecurities and guilt and worry, and says, 'Hey, look, over here. There's another way to do this.' And that way is being kind. The fact you are about to read *The Kindness Method* makes my heart soar. I couldn't have thought of a more perfect name for Shahroo's work.

From the beginning, I was caught off guard. We met in a swanky coffee shop in central London, in broad daylight. It felt almost audacious compared to the hidden-away church basement of a Moderation Management group I'd once attended. And, most startlingly, *we weren't actually talking about wine*. Instead, Shahroo wanted to know my hopes, ambitions; what I thought my skills and talents and strengths were. I was expecting her to ask me to keep a diary of every time I had a glass of Pinot. Instead, she wanted me to note the things that made me, me. Using her maps, the ones you'll find in this book, I began to build a picture of what I wanted my life to look like and what the hurdles to me getting there really were – something I would come back to over time, serving as both an exercise in honesty and a reminder of how far I'd come over the course of our work together.

At first, however, I couldn't quite join the dots. I still kept bringing it back to wine. Over one of our coffees I became despondent: 'Why did I get so drunk at that dinner party at the weekend?!'. Shahroo's response was not to ask me about how much I'd had to drink, but instead, how the dinner party had *made me feel* and in doing so, we uncovered feelings of self-doubt and inadequacy. Through Shahroo's guilt-free probing, I soon realised that drinking wasn't really about the wine (which is precisely why we weren't talking about it); instead, drinking was like an oxygen mask I'd wear, inhaling gasps of extra confidence to take me through situations or emotions I didn't believe I was capable of. And in that way, Shahroo's work isn't about any substance or any habit in particular, be it wine, drugs, gambling, sex or food. These are merely the symptoms; Shahroo's work is about the root cause.

As you will see throughout this book, a lot of Shahroo's work is examining a situation and showing it to you from an entirely different angle. 'Imagine this is an alien looking down at the world of Marisa,' she'd say. It's not often we are able to find the headspace, or time, to look at ourselves from a removed viewpoint. But for that hour, over a coffee, suddenly there were Shahroo and I, looking at how 'Marisa' had behaved that week. This book will give you the tools to find some of that distance, too.

In that space, Shahroo's talent is not to tell you what you've done wrong, but to guide you to a realisation of why that scenario might have played out in the first place. She once described it like ballroom dancing. You, the client, have got to feel like you're the one leading the dance, but she's the one who can actually see where you're going. And once you begin to be able to see those events from a different angle, not only can you begin to really understand your behaviour, but you can start being compassionate towards the person exhibiting those behaviours – the way you would be if it were a friend or even a stranger, basically anyone but you. *The Kindness Method* isn't about Shahroo being kind to you; it's about giving *yourself* the permission to be kind to you. Instead of shame and fear and guilt and disappointment, it's about forcing change with a power too easily overlooked: compassion.

Sometimes our sessions would leave me teary eyed in Fitzrovia Square, facing previously buried truths. Sometimes they'd leave me buoyant and empowered. Unfailingly, however, they always took me one step closer to understanding why I was drinking the way I was drinking. Writing letters to myself – a method advocated in the book – is one of the things that worked well for me. As suggested by Shahroo in one of our sessions, if I wanted to go out for drinks, but wanted to make sure I wasn't there all night, I should write a note of all the nice things I was going to do for myself in the morning. I'd keep the letter in my purse and set an alarm for 10pm. When the alarm went off, I'd scuttle off to the ladies, read the letter and remember why it was time to go home. Drinking less in order to have a nice Saturday morning might not sound like rocket science but, as I was learning, *The Kindness Method* is about allowing yourself to become a priority in your own life. For some of us, that really is quite revelatory.

There's something that makes Shahroo's insights very valid, and that's the variety of clients she's worked with. From the young women of Amy's Place, a recovery house for women, to private high-flying clients or intrigued individuals at the School of Life, it's hugely comforting to know Shahroo understands that behavioural issues are the most human of things that impact us all – even her. Shahroo's frankness about her own weight loss, of which she talks throughout *The Kindness Method*, makes you realise even the wisest of souls have their demons. In fact, maybe that's precisely why they are so wise.

Shahroo used a phrase that had a big impact on a cynical person like me. She told me that it's 'not so much about finding yourself' – a phrase that often makes my eyes roll – 'but about meeting yourself'. If I began the sessions with Shahroo as an alien, looking at Marisa and wondering why on earth she was behaving that way, by the end of those coffees, I'd met Marisa, just as I'm sure you'll have met yourself by the end of this book. Because part of Shahroo's *Kindness Method* is removing harmful, negative narratives we tell ourselves about ourselves and, instead, introducing ourselves to who we *really* are; revealing the traits we actually possess, our strengths and talents, the person buried under all of those nasty myths. Shahroo and I battled past my belief that I was lazy (not true, one summer I had three part-time jobs as student); that I was a bit stupid (not true, I have an MA in 20th-Century Literature); that a drinking habit was inevitable because of family addiction (scientifically, not true); that I was a chaotic mess who couldn't do anything (not true, Shahroo would point out that I was managing to keep a job, write this feature and turn up for coffee on time every week). Through the mapping, via the coffees, some figurative ballroom dancing, a lot of honesty, and a lot of holding Marisa up to the light, I could see none of these narratives was based in fact. And therefore, not only did I have no reason to punish myself, but finally, aged thirty-one, I'd met Marisa. That secret back door to your mind that Shahroo knows the way to is like a backstage pass to who you are; a behind-the-scenes look at what is really going on.

The Kindness Method is a book for those who want to make a quietly revolutionary change to their life; a sustained, lasting change led by honesty and compassion. Through Shahroo's techniques, and the repositioning of how you see yourself, you can become the person you want to be. And crucially, you won't transform in a *Stars in Their Eyes* puff of smoke, instantaneously appearing from a sliding door as the impersonation of someone else. But in time you'll get closer to the happier, healthier, real you, because perhaps for the first time in a long time, or maybe even for the first time ever, you'll start being kind to yourself. Shahroo's power is bewitching; it might not be delivered with a booming voice of revelation (actually, it's delivered from a very glamorous, glossy-maned, young woman) but two years on from those coffees, you'll still find me in the pub on Sunday afternoons but never a Monday night. And while the life-changing conversation Shahroo got me to have is an ongoing one, she started a crucial open dialogue, like an internal peace negotiator between me and myself. When I find myself at a bar now, a small voice suggests putting tonic and ice in glass of wine, because I deserve to be hangover-free on a Saturday morning. I've replaced a 'Why bother? I'm lazy and chaotic anyway', with 'That's enough for me. I've got important things to do tomorrow.' A quiet change to the outside world but revolutionary to me and my life.

I don't believe it's a coincidence that Shahroo's book has landed in the world in 2018. Kindness is without doubt something the world needs so very much right now. If we could start by being kind to ourselves, I'm sure we could be kind to others. The first thing to do right now though, is to find a notepad and pen. It's time to map out the person you want to be.

Marisa Bate

INTRODUCTION

How many times have you embarked on a plan of change, only to run out of steam within weeks? How often do you notice habits emerging that you're not particularly proud of? Maybe you'd like to drink less or exercise more. Maybe you want to stick to a diet or stop putting off a big career change. Have you ever asked yourself the question: 'Why, even though I know it is in my best interests, do I not manage to stick to my plans?'

It doesn't matter what habits you'd like to change or what resolutions you want to stick to – I'm going to show you how to do it. I'll start you on a process that will not only help you put your plans into action but will simultaneously increase your self-esteem, raise your self-awareness and strengthen your resilience. The tools in this book will set you up to have the best possible chance of achieving any goal of your choosing.

I believe that we already know what works for us and what will get us to where we want to be. We just need to follow a simple framework that helps us draw that wisdom out. *The Kindness Method* is not a replacement for diet plans or therapy, for detoxes or 'organise your life' apps. They can all be part of the process if you'd like them to be. This book will simply help you to understand why, time and time again, when you start a new plan, you may be able to keep it up for a while, but you don't quite manage to stick to it. It will also give you some tips on how to create a plan that is sustainable.

Just as if you were attending sessions with me, I will guide you through an easy-to-follow series of exercises designed to help you shine a light on the thoughts and behaviours that are holding you back. The exercises include writing letters to yourself, brainstorming to create personalised memory aids and populating 'maps', and are designed to help you become aware of the ways you may be sabotaging your own efforts. These tools are the ones I use on myself, as well as with my clients.

When I say maps, I simply mean a theme written in the middle of a page, around which you make notes in whatever way suits you (I will go into more detail on how to do this for yourself later in the book). Some of the maps used in substance-misuse treatment are quite prescriptive themselves, and prompt you to answer questions leading on from each other. Some provide headings and fields to complete, with a scoring system at the bottom to keep a track of which maps were most useful. To be honest, most of the maps I've done are free-maps, on blank paper. I will usually pick up from a conversation what is most important for a client to explore during a session, and create a 'map' by writing few words in the middle of a page. I then hand it to them and they develop this however they like, noting down the words and sentences that come to them in whatever order and grouping they like. So, without guidance around how to make them effective, the maps are literally a word or sentence in the middle of a page, around which you make notes randomly.

Although *The Kindness Method* process itself can be applied to address a range of unwanted habits, most of the anecdotal stories and examples in this book are about experiences with drugs (including alcohol and sugar). Not only is this where the bulk of my knowledge and experience lies, but now, in private practice, at least 80 per cent of clients come to talk about alcohol. Attempting to manage a relationship with an addictive substance that alters us chemically poses a range of additional challenges. So I believe that those who have mastered it have an enormous amount to teach us about managing less 'harmful' day-to-day habits.

About Me

Having studied Psychosocial Sciences and then Psychology, my first experience of working in the healthcare field was as an Assistant Psychologist at an NHS substance-misuse service in North West London. During this placement, I learned an enormous amount about how drug addiction is treated in the UK.

I went on to work in frontline community substance-misuse treatment, and I was trained in the core approaches such as Motivational Interviewing*, Relapse Management, Group Facilitation, Risk Management, Brief Intervention, Harm Reduction, Strengths-based Assessment and Mindfulness-based Relapse Prevention. In 2012 I started working for a consultancy, where I learned about commissioning, policy, clinical governance and the political landscape of drug treatment in the UK. Eventually I combined and adapted what I had learned to create my own approach to habit change.

My professional experiences enabled me to observe first-hand what kind of tools were genuinely working for a diverse range of people in different contexts. Still, I wouldn't have been able to share them widely in good conscience had they not passed the ultimate test: working on me. Luckily, they did. After more than two decades of struggling with compulsive overeating and extreme dieting, desperately trying to find a plan I could sustain, I used the tools in this book to lose – and keep off – eight stone.

This wasn't the first time I had lost a lot of weight, but it was the first time I also began to feel more confident and capable across a whole range of areas in my life. That's because, alongside implementing new eating and exercise plans, I simultaneously explored and addressed the challenges I'd been experiencing with my other related patterns around co-dependency, anxiety, low self-

* Motivational Interviewing (MI) was developed by William R. Miller, PhD, and Stephen Rollnick, PhD. According to Miller and Rollnick, 'MI is a collaborative, person-centered form of guiding to elicit and strengthen motivation for change'. *Motivational Interviewing*, third edition, New York, Guilford Press, 2012)

esteem, a need for constant external validation, a lack of boundaries and negative self-talk. I began to understand why my habits had emerged and why I was finding it so hard to change.

About You

I won't be telling you what your goals 'should' be. Your goals are none of my (or anyone else's) business. As far as I'm concerned, you can use this process to do more of something that most people want to do less of, if that's what works for you.

We will all have times throughout our lives when we want to shed unwanted habits that have somehow crept up on us, times when we want to 'check in' and set new goals for ourselves. It's impossible to guess what plans we'll struggle to activate and keep up in five years' time. The beauty of *The Kindness Method* is that each time your goals change, you'll have a wealth of personalised resources (the maps and exercises in this book) available to refer to. That way, at every stage of your life, when you take stock and think, 'I don't like this, I'd like to change it,' you're ready to do so. And you will be able to do this autonomously, armed with tangible reminders of how capable you really are.

My clients come to me because they want to find a way to manage their unwanted habits. These can be around alcohol, food, procrastination, gaming, gambling, sex, overspending, social media, or negative self-talk. Sometimes they're concerned with more than one habit; sometimes many of them together. They often expect me to tell them what they 'should' and 'shouldn't' do and to chastise them for how 'bad' they are compared to my other clients. They want me to tell them what the 'right' goals are and what their reasons for changing should be. This is not how I work, and it is not what *The Kindness Method* is about. Both personal and professional experience have shown me that presuming to know people better than they know themselves and telling them what to do is simply not effective. It can also make them defensive and dishonest – two things that can really slow down the change process.

I don't want you to 'hand yourself over' to me. I want to show you how to formulate plans that are completely tailor-made to your own bespoke needs. My job is simply to guide you, simplify some common motivational concepts, share some tools and teach you how to draw out what you need to know to get to wherever you want to be.

You will set your own goals, safe in the knowledge that the exercises in *The Kindness Method* have no judgement about what's most important to you.

What's It All About?

You will start by documenting what you're good at, and reminding yourself of all the times you've proven that you can feel driven, capable and motivated. You will then start examining the thoughts and behaviours that may be holding you back. I'll invite you to try out new habits and you'll find yourself beginning to naturally observe and pre-empt what unique triggers and situations are likely to throw you off track with your plan. Instead of avoiding the situations that ordinarily result in you 'falling off the wagon', you will reframe them as challenges that you will face head-on and overcome.

Some of these maps and exercises will become part of your regular commitment to increasing your self-esteem, self-efficacy and self-awareness. Some are only relevant to the specific changes you want to make at any given time.

From the moment you start completing the first exercise, you will have started a collection of observations about yourself and your behaviours that will inform the choices you will make for years to come.

By getting to know yourself better, preparing for the hard times ahead and facing them with confidence, you will challenge the core beliefs you have about how capable you are, and start becoming more and more ambitious with your goals. Planning autonomously won't mean excluding other people or resources from the process. It will mean deciding who and what you employ to support you in a considered way, so that you make the best decisions for you, specifically.

The maps you start making today (you'll be guided through this in detail starting from chapter 5) are the same ones you will return to forever. It is worth investing in a good-quality blank notebook – or several – and even some coloured pens if you like the idea of making your maps colourful. You will gradually develop an important log that not only records your successes, but also serves as a personalised memory aid and a private motivational tool to help keep you on track when times are tough.

How Does It Work?

Across the different areas of my work to date, I've observed that those who stay on track with their challenging change plans in the long term have some key things in common:

- They are really clear on why they want to change
- They change for their own reasons
- They are prepared for their drive to waver from minute to minute, so they put things in place to ensure they stay on track despite this inevitability
- They find it exhilarating to keep surprising themselves and challenging long-held assumptions about what they're capable of and deserve
- They practise kindness towards themselves and others

In *The Kindness Method*, I'll be giving you the information you need without having to sift through too much jargon. In the past, when I would read self-help books, I rarely read one cover to cover. Instead, I would go straight to the chapters that sounded like they'd get me to where I wanted to be most quickly. *The Kindness Method* is designed with the presumption that a lot of people read these kinds of books in the same way that I did.

Addictive Personality or Lack of Planning?

None of us is ever *not* engaging in habits. And when we have unwanted ones, we can't just take them away, we have to replace them. Even if our new habit is just 'doing nothing' instead – that's still a habit.

When we don't do enough planning and self-exploration before trying to change a habit, it can seem like a good option to 'wing it'. Often we decide to just stop doing the 'bad' things and 'white knuckle' through the hard bits, using sheer willpower alone. The problem with this is that we forget our drive will fluctuate, and that even if our habits seem completely counterproductive and useless to us right now, they are (or have been in the past) quite the opposite. This means that at some point, many different thoughts, feelings and situations are likely to throw us off track, especially if we aren't expecting them.

Knowing we shouldn't do something or simply being aware that it's having a negative impact on our lives is not enough to create a sustainable change process – it's not even almost enough. Inevitably, we are then faced with a situation where we're ill-prepared and making decisions from outside of our comfort zone. This is when we're likely to take any opportunity to go back to our old ways, even if just for the relief of defaulting to the status quo and delaying facing fear of the unknown. In addition, we very often fail to diversify the coping strategies, distractions and alternatives we habitually reach for to protect ourselves from the thoughts and feelings we want to avoid. Avoidance can often be a big part of feeling at the mercy of our unwanted habits.

Talking Down

Regardless of what habits you are here to address, I believe that there is one crucial habit we need to conquer to make our plans more likely to work out: the habit of negative self-talk. It can lead us to sabotage our own plans and often manifests itself in the kind of behaviours that throw us off track. At those times when we are 'withdrawing' from our place of comfort – whatever that means to each of us – we need to expect that there will be moments when none of the valid reasons we have to change will seem to matter. What's more, the excuses we will make in order to revert to our old ways (or even to pick up new, unwanted habits to relieve stress, boredom or other states we want to avoid) will be creative and convincing and seem appealingly logical.

We need to learn why it suits us to stay the same.

That's why a core part of *The Kindness Method* focuses on listening in on the messages you give yourself. It also encourages you to develop conscious appreciation of how and why it might suit you to stay the same. It also assumes that, no matter how motivated you feel at any given moment, there will be times when all that fades into nothing, and (at least in the short term, before the process becomes second nature and you have time under your belt), you will need tangible memory aids to remind you what you're capable of and how important it is for you to change.

It's the Thought that Counts

The thing that most substance-misuse practitioners have in common, regardless of their therapeutic approach, is that they rarely focus on the actual substance itself that is being misused. They know that creating lasting change isn't really about addressing the substance. It is about learning to cultivate and strengthen a curious and compassionate approach to physical cravings through mindful self-awareness. It is about learning to be discerning about the thoughts you allow to dictate your behaviours. And so these same approaches from drug treatment can be applied to address a range of unwanted day-to-day behaviours.

For example, procrastination may be the habit you're here to change, but it's the ongoing conversations you have with yourself about your plan to stop procrastinating and what it means about you that are important. If those aren't addressed, you will likely find yourself slipping back into old ways.

Rock Bottom

The traditional thinking in addiction treatment was that people didn't change until things got really bad. They had to feel pretty awful about their lives before they made lasting changes, and their habits would have to cause major, unmanageable problems for them to activate a challenging plan to change and stick to it. For some people, this is the case. They are able to describe the moment they decided to change for good, and they've stuck to a plan without ever deviating. They've never looked back because the thought of returning to that 'rock bottom' is enough to keep them on track.

Most of the people I've worked with, however (especially those with more day-to-day unwanted habits), can, over time, normalise the moments when they were most upset with their unwanted habits and declared, 'That's it forever.' Plus, thinking back to those many mini 'rock bottoms' creates an uncomfortable visual they want to quickly push away, but not one that is so frightening that just the prospect of returning to it is enough to keep them on track.

So, with the exception of those who had just one definitive 'rock bottom', I've observed that focusing on what we *don't* want to be or do can get us going and provide much needed perspective, but it doesn't keep us going. For the most part, staying changed isn't about moving away from things we don't want, it's about moving towards what we do want. It's not about punishing ourselves with reminders of how bad things were or could be again, but exciting ourselves with thoughts of how much better things will keep getting. It's about rewarding, accepting, forgiving and understanding ourselves.

Whether we like it or not, the habits we've developed to distract ourselves from our uncomfortable thoughts and feelings have, at some point, been effective and useful – otherwise we wouldn't have clung to them for so long. On balance, they might not be helpful any more, or perhaps they no longer fit into the lives we want to have. Or maybe we just want better, more effective strategies that don't replace one discomfort with another. But the habits in themselves are not 'bad' – and neither are we. From a practical, habit-change perspective, the problem with taking a punitive approach to ourselves and our behaviours is that it reinforces this idea that we're weak and deserving of punishment. This attitude does not put us in the mindset we need to be in to keep going with our plans when it's most difficult to.

When we regard our plans as a punishment we've had to impose on ourselves it's much more tempting to rebel. *The Kindness Method* is not about saying, 'I've been bad and weak, I can't believe I've turned out this way, I need fixing.' It's about saying, 'I'm fine as I am, but I choose to learn more about my thoughts and behaviours, and improve – for my own reasons.' Plus, when you identify how your thoughts and behaviours were (or still are) serving you, you will gain invaluable insight into what alternative long-term coping strategies would suit you specifically.

Expert by Experience

The field of addiction recovery widely acknowledges the wisdom of 'experts by experience' – people who've been there before us and done it. I am writing *The Kindness Method* partly as a practitioner, but mainly as an expert by experience.

I used to believe myself to be one of those 'all or nothing' people, someone who couldn't stick to a plan or ever really learn to moderate anything. As a result, I battled a problem with my weight my entire life. I've tried all the fad diets under the sun and paid out a lot of money to the newest guru, the latest coach, health camps – you name it, I've done it. Every Monday I would start a new, extreme plan. For years, I punished myself for my weakness by starving myself for periods of time and then bingeing. I would isolate myself until I was 'thin enough' to go out, spending Sunday evenings with a slice of pizza in one hand and a registration form for yet another miracle boot camp or juicing plan in the other – one that I was determined would 'fix' me for good this time. One thing's for sure, I knew how to lose weight. In fact, I was very skilled at understanding how to lose a lot of weight very quickly.

There have never been more effective diets available to us, and I believe that they can absolutely work. For me, finding a plan to subscribe to was never the problem. Keeping the weight off and actually feeling comfortable in myself, however, was a different matter.

Now that I know what I know about changing my own habits, I've identified why so often it took me months, or even years, to get going and why my 'relapses' were so catastrophic:

- I didn't truly believe in my ability to change my behaviour permanently
- I wasn't being honest with myself or others about some of the reasons I wanted to change
- I approached change as a punishment for weakness and laziness
- I wasn't prepared for how difficult it would be
- I zoomed in on my 'bad' behaviours, instead of focusing on the life I wanted to move towards

Whatever Gets You There

When I was really overweight, I didn't want to tell the GP I cared more about how I looked in a bikini than whether I was at a higher risk of diabetes. I wasn't proud of it, but in those moments when I desperately wanted to jump off a treadmill, it wasn't the thought of a healthy medical report that would keep me going, it was the prospect of being able to wear jeans with buttons again.

We're often told what 'should' be motivating us and reasons we 'should' want to change. We're constantly reminded of what is wrong with our habits. Everyone knows what's harmful about alcohol or overeating. But when I'd hear warnings from well-meaning, knowledgeable professionals, I wouldn't only hear that there was something wrong with my behaviour, I'd hear that there was something wrong with me. If I knew these habits were impacting so many areas of my life, why was I being so weak? Why couldn't I just change?!

What I now know is that deep down I didn't think I deserved to change. I also didn't have the right tools. I wasn't weak, but I was trapped in a vicious cycle. By applying some of the approaches in *The Kindness Method* to show myself the consideration and compassion that I usually reserved for others, I found a way to break it.

CHAPTER 1
A-HA! MOMENTS
___

As a compulsive, stubborn person who always took things to extremes, I decided that if I could create a programme that worked on me, it could work on other people, too. Of course, I already had a programme I was working to – we all do. However you're behaving right now can be seen as the 'programme' you've developed over time. Adopting *The Kindness Method* is about changing your current programme to one you've consciously and willingly created.

In my case, when it came to creating a programme that helped me explore my specific habits, I wanted it to be a private process. I also wanted to feel like I was in charge of the plan. I would definitely need a clear framework to follow, and this time it needed to help me feel better about how I was 'doing life', as opposed to just being about my dress size. I had managed to lose weight before, but because my self-esteem remained so low, it never gave me any sustained feeling of wellbeing. It was also very short lived and didn't improve any other areas of my life. The exhausting disappointment of this realisation, over and over again, was enough to set me on a cycle of relapse and leave me heavier and more disillusioned each time.

I owe the new 'programme' that works for me now to a range of professional and personal experiences I had. They helped me to understand why I was trapped in a cycle, and gave me the insight I needed to create an approach that could help a wide range of people help themselves. I'd like to share with you some realisations that helped me develop the key elements of *The Kindness Method*. These are my 'a-ha!' moments – in no particular order.

First Experience
Attending Overeaters Anonymous meetings

First Realisation
We're all perfectly capable of identifying our own particular needs – provided we have a clear framework to guide us

I wanted to be knowledgeable about where I was sending my clients for further support in the community and so I attended mutual-aid groups, where non-professionals with something in common would gather, share their experiences and help each other to stay on track with their plan. I knew that fellowships like Alcoholics Anonymous were proving effective in helping people in the long term and so I went along to learn more.

I would sit in awe among groups of people who had managed to stop drinking by committing to a model specifically designed to help them achieve recovery. In this context, that meant they would endeavour to never touch their substances of abuse again.

There are similar twelve-step groups available to address separate behaviours that are so often interlinked, that use the same learned framework. For example, some of my clients who are years into abstinent recovery from alcohol will start to attend groups to address their behaviours around sex or co-dependency, using a framework and programme that already works for them.

During the period when I'd started attending these groups to learn more for work, I discovered there was a twelve-step group called 'Overeaters Anonymous', or OA. Naturally, it interested me on a personal level. Having settled into a norm of constant bingeing, negative self-talk and social isolation, it was around this time that I found myself at my heaviest. So, I went to OA.

To my surprise, I was clearly the most overweight person there by a long way. But this wasn't a weight-loss group at all. I discovered that some of the people there had never been overweight at all, but nonetheless their reliance on food had made their lives unmanageable. I was surrounded by people who had been able, just like those in Alcoholics Anonymous, to find 'recovery' by adopting a specific programme. But one thing was different about this group: you can't be abstinent from food. You have to eat. I was surrounded by a new type of self-labelled addict, the kind that has to handle and consume their substance of abuse every day. This meant that everyone in the OA group had developed awe-inspiring levels of self-awareness.

> No one talked about carbs or calories, as I was used to.
> Here they talked about emotions and self-esteem and
> resilience.

The people at OA had identified which particular types of food would send them spiralling into their personal definition of 'relapse'. Even though they all followed a traditional abstinence-based framework, each had a very personal definition of what recovery meant to them. No one talked about carbs or calories, as I was used to from some of the previous weight-loss groups I'd attended. Here they talked about emotions, self-esteem and resilience. The stories they shared about the lengths they had gone to for their dependency were often as shocking and humbling as those I had heard from people with alcohol dependencies.

One thing common to those who are in recovery from types of addiction where they don't wish to, or can't, abstain altogether is that they have clearly defined what their own 'bottom lines' are. These are behaviours that they have identified as being harmful to their recovery, either for a defined stage of the process or for the rest of their lives. Any behaviours they engage in that fall below these bottom lines are considered a lapse or relapse. Everyone's are different, just as are everyone's triggers. The wisdom I picked up from OA helped me enormously to create a weight-loss plan that finally worked for me. One of the main differences between this plan and the ones that had failed before was that I set myself non-negotiable 'bottom lines'. In the initial stages of change, I defined myself as being in 'recovery' if I was abstaining from the specific foods that I had never before been able to eat in moderate quantities. (Some of them were very healthy foods, but for some reason they always seemed to start a spiral into a massive binge.)

Second Experience
Working with clients who have been given court orders to attend sessions with me for substance-misuse treatment

Second Realisation
Shifting the focus from prescriptive outcomes to holistic wellbeing can naturally push out unwanted behaviours

One of my most interesting roles in drug treatment involved working with people who were required by law to complete Drug Rehabilitation Requirements (DRRs). This sort of sentence is appropriate for 'problem drug users' who are seen to be committing crimes to fund their drug habit. Depending on the 'level' of the DRR they were given, they would need to show up between one and three times a week and be willing work with me to address their substance misuse, and they would also have to be tested for drugs. It was my responsibility to report back to probation services on how they were doing. Failure to stick to their recovery plan would mean they would have to return to court for breaching their order. This could then result in re-sentencing, which could mean prison.

The clients I was working with here were not those who believed they had 'hit rock bottom'. They had not walked in off the street, asking for help. They could be seen as being coerced into treatment. Nevertheless, most of these clients still successfully completed their orders and effectively addressed their substance misuse. A lot of the time they simply hadn't been aware of what support was available to them or didn't know any other way of living, having grown up in environments where substance abuse was the norm.

One client really stood out for me and taught me a great deal. According to his court reports, he had been caught repeatedly shoplifting because he was a dependent drug user who couldn't otherwise afford to fund his habit. He had agreed to engage in treatment to address his drug use and as such was required to attend weekly sessions with me over six months. My overall tasks were to work with him on his general motivation levels to attend sessions (which were notably high) and help him to provide negative drug-test results (which he always did). In fact, from the very first session we had, his drug-test results came up negative – and continued to do so every single week after that.

As I guided him through the process of filling out maps and using motivational tools aimed at increasing his confidence to change drug-using behaviours, I noticed he had notably high levels of self-belief from the off. It became more and more clear that he had a range of practical, social and financial resources available to him. He also had three phones that would ring continuously throughout our sessions. Very often, he'd have to excuse himself to have brief conversations, asking the person on the other end of the line to call back when our session had ended.

Wary of making unfair assumptions, for the first couple of months I continued to work with this client as though he was indeed, until apparently very recently, a heavily dependent, regular drug user. As per the procedure, I often discussed this client with more experienced colleagues in multidisciplinary team meetings and supervision sessions. They shared my suspicions: that perhaps this man had been caught in possession of illegal drugs not because he was a drug user, but rather because he was a drug dealer. This was naturally discussed with the other services involved in the client's care but there was little evidence to support our suspicions and frankly, no well-meaning, hardworking practitioner or health and social care worker wants to say, 'This client is doing too well, and that's a problem.' So I continued to meet with him every week.

I reasoned that the ideal outcome for my work with this client was the same that the courts, the probation services and the substance-misuse services would have. We all wanted him to be a productive member of society; one who wasn't engaging in illegal behaviours that put him or others in danger. So I had an idea. Whether he was a dealer or a user or both, what if I could work with him to decrease the likelihood of him having to turn up for sessions with people like me in the long term? What if he could feel capable of creating a life he preferred to the one he had now? It couldn't be enjoyable to deal with criminal justice services and constantly answer telephone calls asking him to run from one place to another. I couldn't imagine he thought he could sustain this lifestyle into old age.

So I shifted the focus. I started talking to him about the kind of life he wanted to have. We discussed the qualities of the people he respected, and reflected on what he had wanted to be when he was younger. We talked about the hobbies he had neglected along the way, and where he saw his life in five and in ten years' time. We explored with excitement what he'd do if his 'relationship with drugs' was out of the picture.

Surprisingly quickly, things started changing. First, he became very interested in life-planning during our sessions and visualising his professional ambitions. He started playing football again. Eventually, he signed up for an internship programme where he would learn to fix bikes (as I discovered he'd loved to do as a teenager). He managed to get a job that kept him busy from nine till five and left him too exhausted to do much else in the evenings. He began to use our sessions to plan the company he wanted to set up for himself (all the while demonstrating that he had a wealth of skills in relationship building, cash-flow projection and debt management).

By the end of his six-month order, he had just one phone, which barely rang. He was excited about his life and, although I suppose I'll never know for sure, I suspect that his involvement with illegal drugs – in whatever form that had been in reality – had stopped. Which meant that the courts, along with a lot of other services, were happy. And from a professional standpoint, so was I.

> *To really change our unwanted behaviours, we need to 'zoom out' and focus on the entire life we want to live.*

This experience taught me that in order to really change our unwanted behaviours, we need to 'zoom out' and focus on the entire life we want to live. We can let small achievements fuel our belief that we can surprise ourselves with what we are capable of. When we can get excited about who we want to be on a bigger scale, the habits that fit into our ideal lives will follow naturally and the ones that don't serve us any more will gradually get pushed out. By taking this approach, we can avoid the scary, 'empty' withdrawal period, when the way we've always known has been taken away from us before we've replaced it with countless better things.

Third Experience
Learning about drug markets on the dark net

Third Realisation
We all need places where we can honestly explore the thoughts and behaviours we're not proud of, without fear of judgement

In 2014 I had just started to apply what I knew about addiction to my weight loss. Progress had been slow and I was acutely aware that there was a long road ahead. One evening, when I felt at risk of a self-sabotaging binge, I decided I would go out to learn something new until the cravings and possibility of a lapse had passed.

And so it was that I attended a talk at Goldsmiths University by Jamie Bartlett, who was speaking about a book he had written entitled *The Dark Net*. I had absolutely no idea what to expect. During the talk we were introduced to 'The Silk Road', an online marketplace where people could buy and discuss illegal drugs pretty much anonymously. I was really surprised to see how similar the site looked to ones I was familiar with, like Amazon. Sellers and their drugs were honestly reviewed and there were forums where people would openly share their experiences of commonly stigmatised behaviours.

At this time, I was working as a frontline substance-misuse worker, and I already had my suspicions that the process my clients had to go through to seek help did not encourage them to be completely honest about the realities of how they were procuring and administering illegal drugs.

In the UK, if you feel you have a problem with alcohol or other drugs, you can go to a local substance-misuse treatment centre and ask for help. Of course each service is different, and there have been improvements in recent years, but for the most part, this is how the process goes:

- You walk in and ask someone for help
- You're asked to sit and wait for an assessor, often surrounded by posters about the dangers of overdose
- If you can be seen that day, an assessor will take you into a private room and explain that before you can get help, they will need to complete some forms on your behalf by asking you a series of questions
- You will be told that you need to sign contracts agreeing that, if you share anything that the service deems is a risk to yourself or others, your details could be passed on to social services, DVLA, the police and other authorities
- The assessment begins. First you're typically asked to share (among many other things) your address, information about any children you may have, your occupation, mental- and physical-health diagnoses and details of any previous or current involvement with criminal justice
- Then you're asked for an honest account of what stigmatised (often illegal) behaviours you are engaging in

I always suspected that the information people gave about themselves was at best censored and at worst completely inaccurate. I know I certainly wouldn't want to tell a stranger how much I was drinking if I had children I was driving to school, let alone if I was buying illegal drugs, for fear that I would be reported to the authorities. Practitioners have told me that, much further into the treatment process (provided the client has come back), they often discover that the person seeking help hadn't been completely – or often even nearly – truthful in this initial assessment.

Furthermore, the traditional substance-misuse assessment is a very deficit-based process, in that it focuses on the problems to be addressed. It is designed this way to help safely assess and manage risk, as well as to be able to pass on important information to other agencies who might be involved with a client's treatment. But from the point of view of the person being assessed, it is a forty-five-minute to one-hour experience of going through everything that is 'wrong' with them. I've often said that if someone didn't want to use drugs before an assessment, they would certainly want to afterwards.

So, how does this relate to the dark net? If the assessment process discouraged honesty and therefore potentially hindered treatment, I found the possibility that people could have the freedom to anonymously discuss behaviours around their use of illegal drugs extremely interesting.

After attending the talk, I immediately started reading dark-net user forums and quickly learned that what I was being told during substance-misuse assessments 'above ground' was often a world away from what was really going on. On some forums, people were sharing experiences on how they managed to gain control of problematic drug use, swapping tips and providing support to each other openly. Anonymity helped people start from where they actually were when it came to their drug use, not from where they wanted to be perceived as being by others.

Exploring these and similar forums served not only to make me a more effective and knowledgeable practitioner, it also drew my attention to a major need: a space for people to explore and be completely truthful about habits they are not proud of, without fear of judgement or punishment from friends, family, peers, authorities or society. That's what I hope this book can provide.

> *Everyone needs a place where they can be honest about what they are thinking and doing and why they are doing it, without fear of judgement or punishment from friends, family, peers, authorities or society.*

Fourth Experience
Training addiction workers in motivational concepts

Fourth Realisation
The same tools that can help people come off highly addictive drugs can help the general population to manage their day-to-day habits

During my career in community substance-misuse services, I have been trained in different methods used in the health and social care sector to help bring about change in those who were most resistant to it. One of the trainers I had, Ray Jenkins, really stood out. He is an extremely engaging and knowledgeable facilitator who has worked in the field for over thirty years. I found he had a clear, no-nonsense way of explaining how to use a range of therapeutic tools. He knew all the evidence-base around which approaches were working and he wasn't afraid to say which ones weren't.

I had been encouraged to use maps as a therapeutic tool with clients; however, it was Ray's training that taught me to adopt the spirit behind them, and made me see how I could guide people to engage with the maps as a meaningful exercise in self-discovery, rather than a tick-box exercise.

Ray hired me to work with him as a trainer and eventually a consultant. I was delighted to learn that he took the same approach when he was motivating me as a staff member that I'd learned about in his substance-misuse training courses. He focused on strengths and values and helped build my resilience, so that I started viewing areas for improvement as new challenges, not the earth-shattering crises they would have been before.

Working with Ray, I began to train experienced healthcare professionals in how to help motivate people in addiction to move on from services and thrive in the community. For three years I travelled around the UK, teaching frontline workers how to use mapping most effectively. At first I pretty much copied Ray but eventually I found my own style.

Initially I set up my training sessions so that the delegates would work through the maps and exercises with certain clients in mind. But I found that, more and more, the staff were asking me for extra maps. Eventually I twigged that the people I was training were using these maps on themselves – for smoking, eating, procrastinating, getting angry with their partners – any behaviours they wanted to change! Soon I started actively asking people to use the maps on themselves, assuring them they wouldn't have to show them to anyone else. Not only did they get more from the training, it meant they bought in more to the approach. Their feedback on what was clear and useful and what wasn't also helped me tweak the process. Plus, they could now promote the process to their clients, who, instead of waiting for their next weekly keyworking session, could start taking maps away and taking sustained habit change into their own hands – first for their concerns around drugs, and then for anything else they wanted to change.

Eventually I twigged that the people I was training were using these maps on themselves – for smoking, eating, procrastinating, getting angry with their partners – any behaviours they wanted to change!

Fifth Experience
Seeing a counsellor

Fifth Realisation
Being kind to yourself, regardless of whether or not you can achieve your goals, actually helps you achieve them more quickly

A few years ago I started seeing a counsellor after a break-up that I was finding particularly hard to move on from. Over the course of the three-and-a-half-year relationship, I had gained over seven stone and lost a lot of self-esteem. But this time I just didn't have the energy to create another 'dramatic transformation' while I was, frankly, so low. I decided I would get some counselling and then go about my usual extreme diet and exercise plan so that I could make myself 'worthy' of going out and engaging with the world again.

I wish I could tell you that I approached counselling as an opportunity to systematically work through my issues around co-dependency, low self-esteem and abandonment, all of which were contributing to my unhealthy relationship with food. After all, I work in psychology, so my logical head knew that this was what counselling was for. But in reality, I mainly saw counselling as a new 'solution', the effectiveness of which I'd ultimately only be measuring in stones shed.

One day, after spending another half an hour slumped in the counselling chair looking like I hadn't seen a mirror in weeks, I described in detail how energetic and happy I intended to be in a year's time, when I'd take pride in my appearance and sit up straight and 'be slim and happy'. The counsellor asked a very simple question that really shook me – one that I had never considered in my entire life: *'How about if you're never slim? What would happen if you just stayed this size for the rest of your life?'* The anger that ran through me was unlike any I'd ever experienced towards someone trying to help. 'How dare she?!' I thought. How could she think it would be okay for me to feel this way for the rest of my life? I'm paying her to make me feel happier and she's suggesting that I could be happy without achieving the one goal that I know will solve every problem in my life.

I spent a few days flitting between rage about what the counsellor had said and drafting break-up texts with her (which were very much taking an 'it's not me, it's absolutely YOU' tone). Then, as the anger started to subside, I allowed myself to dip a toe into her suggestion. In a world where I would never lose weight, would I want to continue being cruel to myself and living life 'on hold'? I looked around and saw other people who were overweight and I realised I would never speak to them the way I was speaking to myself. I didn't think *they* were undeserving of self-care, I didn't think *they* should isolate themselves and stop socialising. I didn't think *they* looked unattractive or judge *their* value by their size.

At this point, I felt I was so undeserving of any joy because of my weight that I didn't even allow myself to listen to happy music. Feeling 'unworthy' was my place of comfort. I didn't have to go out and face rejection or criticism. Of course, it wasn't how I looked that was holding me back, it was my assumption that looking that way meant I simply had to delay enjoying my life. Somewhere along the way (I've now identified when through mapping), I learned that for as long as I was overweight, I strongly believed I wasn't worthy of even the smallest of day-to-day joys.

I decided to do an experiment. I would start behaving as I had intended to once I had lost the weight I believed I needed to. I would be kinder to myself, because I had presumed that once I was slim what I had achieved would make me 'worthy' of that. I would eat what 'future slim-me' ate to maintain her new lifestyle. I would take pride in my appearance as slim-me would, and engage with the world in a way that this more confident, accomplished, future self would. I would protect my time and notice when I was neglecting my own needs. I would take up opportunities to meet new people and go on dates. Even if it felt like faking, I would actively challenge the assumption that I could only do these things once I was slim.

Strangely enough, when I started to apply this thinking to

everything I did I began to lose weight more quickly and more easily than ever before. As soon as I realised that decreasing numbers on the scales weren't the only measure of whether I was worthy of being kind to myself, the by-product of the kindness happened to be that many areas of my life vastly improved. Weight loss became just one added bonus of me actually living my 'ideal life'.

Sixth Experience
Coaching Marisa Bate

Sixth Realisation
There are a lot of people out there who want to address their relationship with alcohol but don't want to stop altogether and don't know where to go for support

During the summer of 2016, I was contacted by Marisa Bate, a senior editor at *The Pool*, an online magazine designed for women, who had heard about some habit-change workshops I had put on in London. She explained that while she didn't want to stop drinking altogether, her relationship with alcohol was concerning her.

Marisa told me that she'd tried attending some support groups but they weren't suited to her needs. For example, often they were abstinence-focused and other group members were suffering far more severely than she was as a result of their relationships with alcohol. She told me what I had often heard from people who had attended support groups or tried interventions that were designed for those whose lives had become truly unmanageable. This was that attending these groups often made them normalise their behaviours and believe that comparatively their problem 'wasn't that bad'.

So often people decide they will do something about their drinking 'once and for all', while they are hungover or following a particularly negative alcohol-related experience. They then find that after time has passed and their body (and perhaps pride) has recovered, they begin to think, 'It wasn't so bad. I'm not drinking in the morning or losing my home. I was overreacting.'

Marisa and I arranged to meet in a coffee shop for casual, one-hour discussions to explore her concerns. She would then write a series of articles about her experience of our work together. There was no need for our conversations to become highly personal. Instead, we talked about why some people are always the last ones at the pub, and how interesting it is that we often associate drinking with giving us confidence, yet although we grow more confident in a range of ways as we get older, we don't decrease the amount we drink in response. Through these conversations, Marisa was able to explore her own patterns and gain insight into what was making it difficult for her to change on her own. Together we formulated some realistic plans for her to try out and feed back on the following week. We would then tweak the plan according to what worked for her and what didn't, until she found something she was happy to stick to long term.

Marisa's pieces in *The Pool* about our work together were incredibly honest and really resonated with both women and men. Over the days and weeks following the publication of her final article I received so many requests for one-to-one sessions that I set up a private practice with a waiting list.

Seeing how many people had the same concerns as Marisa motivated me to capture what had helped her most, so that others could benefit too. Especially those who felt their habits were becoming problematic but didn't quite require one-to-one sessions with a practitioner.

The Kindness Method

As a result of these 'a-ha!' moments, *The Kindness Method* as a finished product is a private, judgement-free, guided process designed to help people achieve self-defined goals by creating their own bespoke programme, informed by what works.

I know what you're thinking: 'If I have to read chapters that are this long before I get going, I have a while to delay making any actual changes.' Perhaps you're here to look at your relationship with food, alcohol, or any other kind of 'consumption', and you're planning a final binge. If that's the case, all I ask at this stage is that you observe that thought. I don't say this as a professional therapist, I say it as a professional procrastinator and experienced excuse-maker.

CHAPTER 2
LESSONS FROM ADDICTION

——

In this chapter, I'd like to start introducing you to a few of the ideas that proved useful when I was helping myself and my clients to change unwanted habits. Consider it a 'handing over' of valuable things I've stumbled upon over the years, as well as a bit of background on how things work in addiction treatment.

If you're anything like me, I imagine you're ready to get going with the maps. In fact, if you're anything like me, you'll be tempted not to read this chapter at all. But it's important that you do, not least because of the essential information it contains on how to get the most out of the maps and other exercises.

We're Not Weak and We Don't Need Fixing

We all know the formula for losing weight and for getting fitter. We know how to stop our credit-card debt from racking up. We also all know how to stop smoking (the answer is, literally, 'stop smoking'). So of course, when we can't manage to do these things, we think we're weak and incapable. This is despite the fact that most of us are achieving things in daily life that completely invalidate these assumptions about ourselves.

Miracle cures and trendy plans can often provide a quick fix that works at getting us where we want to be but they don't necessarily keep us there. We need to take a deeper approach if we want to sustain change for life. Plus there's no denying that the business models behind a lot of miracle, surface, quick-fix 'cures' rely on us coming back over and over again when we're at our most vulnerable; that is, when we once again feel defeated, weak and in need of 'fixing'.

A problem I have with the suggestion that we need 'fixing' is that by extension it suggests we'll one day be 'fixed'. We know full well we're never done, or we'd be riding high on our achievements, letting them accumulate until we were floating around on a cloud of self-confidence. What we tend to do instead is to normalise our achievements quickly, before worrying about the next thing. This arrival at the elusive state of 'being fixed' never comes about.

Addiction recovery has taught me that when we make big changes from a place of feeling fed up and weak, we get started but we don't always keep going. We need to start feeling better about ourselves to do that. That's why, in *The Kindness Method*, we don't even define our specific plans to change until we're quite far into the process, when we are already feeling confident, capable and full of self-knowledge.

Stand Up to Your Inner Bully

Many of us have adopted unsustainable long-term strategies for being less negatively impacted by uncomfortable thoughts and feelings. Some people attempt to avoid them by using highly addictive drugs which are, at least in the short term, effective blockers. Others try food, shopping, gaming, gambling, sex . . . the list goes on. Other than the obvious harms associated with relying on some of these 'fixes', the underlying feelings remain. If you're immediately and compulsively reaching for something to relieve you, you don't create the time and space required to observe, examine and address the source of the discomfort that you're trying to avoid.

And there's another aspect to this. A lot of the people I've worked with have discovered that much of what they're avoiding is mean internal chatter. Very often, while we are in the process of striving for moments of mental stillness through traditional meditative practice, we observe thought patterns which I call 'conversations with ourselves'. When we focus our observations on our thought patterns and these inner conversations about who we are, what we're capable of and how we see ourselves in the context of specific habits, we can gain some real insight into why we're not making changes. *The Kindness Method* aims to make you feel strong enough to face what you are hearing.

> The Kindness Method *will help you feel strong enough to face up to your inner bully.*

As those conversations you have with yourself gradually become more kind, more curious and more fair, they become easier to listen to. There are fewer 'push–pull' debates constantly running through our minds. When there's less need to expend energy desperately trying to push difficult thoughts away, space is created for a gradual mind–body shift so that what we're hearing gradually becomes how we're feeling. Then our decisions – be they about food, sex or our life purpose – are led by our core values and come from a considered place where we've decided what feels right for us. They're no longer dictated by the internal commands we hear that are based on false assumptions we have about ourselves, and about what we're capable and worthy of.

By using the exercises in *The Kindness Method*, I hope that at any stage of life you are able to re-establish what unique combination of elements makes a decision feel right for you, and be led by that. Regardless of the habit you wish to change, starting from this place will inform the creation of a bespoke practical plan of least resistance, for you, specifically.

The Stories We Tell Ourselves

I often observe that clients fall off track with their plans and 'lapse' or 'relapse' because they've told themselves a story. This story goes that depriving themselves of the thing that turns down the volume of their internal chatter in the short term is actually a punishment. Very often, when I was attempting to lose weight, a relapse would be prompted by the internal question: 'Why am I being cruel to myself by depriving myself of the foods I love?' In the context of changing habits, being kind to yourself is remembering at all times that you deserve to live your best possible life and that if this internal chatter becomes louder in the short term, and discomfort comes about, you can withstand it. In order to get to where you want to be in the long term, you need to be okay with curiously and consciously listening to your self-sabotaging thoughts and willingly feeling your impulses, instead of trying to push them away as soon as they pop up.

The Power of Visible Recovery

There are many reasons why support groups are so therapeutically effective, but one of the most important ones is visible recovery. What this means, in essence, is the power of seeing other people who have been through similar struggles and been successful in achieving their goals. There is also a power and connection gained through shared vulnerability and articulating our experiences out loud.

> *Being able to see and hear other people admitting they have the same conversations going on with themselves, the same self-doubt, the same habit of beating themselves up, can have a profound impact on us.*

In my ideal world we would all regularly attend emotional-support groups where we connect with others; we wouldn't just think of them as a gloomy last resort for those who have terrible, severe problems. We would walk excitedly into 'self-esteem' groups and publicise how proud we are to be dedicating time to becoming more self-aware and kinder to ourselves, the same way we do when we smugly share that we've been to the gym. But I'm a realist and I know that for various reasons people aren't always up for sharing out loud to others, especially about thoughts and behaviours they're less than proud of. So, in place of that, I ask that you use the maps and exercises in

The Kindness Method to be as honest and as vulnerable with yourself as you can; to unpack and declare your internal chatter; to see it set down in black and white so it's real and there for you to observe and challenge. Doing it this way means that you can be absolutely truthful with absolutely no fear of anyone else judging you.

Being Better Than Well

A few years ago, a friend called to ask me for some advice. She'd started dating someone who had revealed he was a recovering alcoholic. He had been attending daily support groups to maintain his abstinent recovery of many years. She wanted to ask whether I thought this admission created any cause for concern. I realised that I'd worked in addiction for so long I'd forgotten how many people aren't aware of what my colleagues and I absolutely know to be true: those in long-term recovery from substance abuse aren't just doing 'not badly', they're not even just 'doing well'. They are doing much better than well.

I knew my friend had found someone who was actively self-aware, emotionally accountable and surrounded by a strong support network. He had probably found a way of living that gave him a greater sense of connection and purpose. He would likely know a lot when it came to coping skills compared to the average person whose habits hadn't at one stage made their lives seem unmanageable.

Those in recovery haven't simply changed one habit, they have changed almost every habit that used to accommodate it. They have managed to change how they speak to themselves. Those in long-term recovery have done what this book is designed to help you do – they've found a programme that works for them and that they can apply across their entire lives.

Addiction Lessons Are Human Lessons

There's a good reason why the modern approaches that work so effectively for those in active addiction are useful to the general population. And that is because, fundamentally, they are personal development tools for living well. The days of taking a 'them and us' attitude to the relationship between drug users and professionals are gone. The tools and literature now used in evidence-based models of substance-misuse treatment are designed to cultivate self-awareness, resilience and emotional intelligence. They encourage accountability, autonomy and self-led change.

Many addiction workers who are not in recovery themselves (or at least not openly) are asked the same question: 'How can you help me if you're not an addict yourself?' During my training sessions, delegate healthcare workers have often asked for my advice on how best to deal with this question. I believe the answer lies in reminding ourselves that we are all human. Just because, for a range of different (and highly debated) reasons, someone has become dependent on physically addictive/illegal substances, it doesn't mean that the core emotions and feelings that they are taking those substances to try to push away are not universal in many ways to all of us.

When I'm faced with scepticism from a client, I ask them to tell me what thoughts and feelings they associate with being trapped in a cycle of addictive behaviour. Common responses include shameful, guilty, bored, resentful, helpless, numb, powerless, hopeless, disappointed, isolated, misunderstood . . . and the list goes on. I assure them that though it may be to varying different degrees, everyone will experience one or all of these things at different life stages.

Assets, Ambivalence and Motivation

As I mentioned before, the old-fashioned approach to change in addiction treatment relied on people being motivated by everything that was wrong with their behaviour – and with themselves.

It focused on deficits, and relied on things getting really unmanageable before people would be able to change, by handing themselves over to 'experts'.

The more modern, 'asset-based' approach to supporting those in active addiction to achieve recovery is very different. Now practitioners know that we need to accept that people will be ambivalent about change and that they can start making positive changes without waiting for things to get worse. We acknowledge, with respect and compassion, that there are reasons for people to stay as they are. We know that first they need to feel like capable, active, worthy participants in the process of making lasting positive changes in their lives. We help them to identify what strengths and resources they have at their disposal to help resolve any ambivalence about changing for good.

In this book I help you to identify the assets you have at your disposal, and support you to believe in your ability to change. I will show you how to formulate a well-thought-out plan and encourage you to take action in a positive, realistic way. Practitioners now know that taking an authoritarian, confrontational approach to people and their habits can mean slowing down the process at best or complete disengagement at worst, so I want to focus on your strengths and achievements, not your deficits and 'failings'. Using a non-judgemental, compassionate approach to try and draw out your values and your internal wisdom is far more effective than telling you what is 'best' and where you've gone wrong in the past. People need to be given options so they can choose what kind of approach suits them best. You will need the space to set your own goals, for your own reasons.

These days, substance-misuse workers see their role as 'walking alongside' clients, and co-producing bespoke recovery plans with them, all the while acknowledging that they will have completely understandable reasons to stay as they are. Working in the community, my main goal wasn't for clients to simply be drug-free or 'managing their use', it was for them to live well in every possible way. From my experience, the most effective substance-misuse practitioners don't impose goals or agendas, they consider the state of people's relationships, work, education, spirituality, personal development, physical health. They know that people should not be reduced to their 'bad' behaviours.

❝ *People should not be reduced to their 'bad' behaviours.*

All these strategies can be applied to addressing your unwanted habits. It's no longer about focusing on the extent of the behaviour you want to change, but rather on your readiness to change. Readiness to change will occur when you identify your genuine reasons for wanting to change, while increasing your belief that you really can, even when you feel unmotivated.

Motivation is not a set state. It will fluctuate according to a range of interactions, thoughts, feelings and experiences. It's not the case that some people are just permanently motivated and others aren't. You will need to prepare for your motivation levels to increase and decrease – often seemingly out of the blue. Most people in long-term recovery will back this up, explaining that sometimes lapses occur mere moments after they've felt the most motivated. Addiction-treatment professionals also know now that even though people ultimately have to make their own changes, practically speaking, there is so much we can do to support them in getting where they want to be. Such as hand over tools like these in *The Kindness Method*.

———

CHAPTER 3
GETTING READY
TO CHANGE

———

Very often, when we have 'had enough' of our unwanted habits, we go straight into the 'action' phase, without spending much time planning for the road ahead. Of course, everyone is different, and for some of us this may work. In my experience, however, it's the planning stages that are the most important for most people. And yet even those who accept this usually focus on 'the plan' itself: for example, how many calories we are going to allow ourselves, how many hours of work – what are the rules and regulations.

While it can be extremely important to be prescriptive in this way about your practical plan (especially in the early stages), *The Kindness Method* is concerned with first working backwards from achieving your goals, and considering the people, situations and thoughts that may throw you off track during the journey towards that. This includes:

- Planning for your self-sabotaging thoughts
- Planning for what you'll do when you most want to give up
- Planning things you can do to distract yourself while urges to go off-plan pass
- Planning to also develop more diverse, sustainable, long-term strategies and approaches
- Pre-preparing maps and letters to yourself that you can refer to at times when you feel most vulnerable

- Deciding on the things you'll say to yourself when you're finding it most difficult to stay on track

The way I see it, if you focus on strategies to develop your general resilience, self-esteem and self-awareness, you're better placed to implement any practical plan you like. This time will be different because you're taking the time to really prepare for this change to last. That's why the practical bit comes after working through a lot of maps and exercises.

> *Change doesn't begin when your everyday life looks different, it begins when you do your first map.*

If you're a quick-fix person like I was, this may annoy you; it sounds a bit like you have to spend ages analysing yourself before you get going and see results. The good news is that you have all the exercises in your hands right now. You don't have to wait for next week's session.

Lapse or Relapse? It's the Conversations Around It that Make All the Difference

When talking about addiction recovery, a lapse can be seen as a speedbump that we quickly get back on track from. A lapse becomes a relapse when either we've returned to how we were behaving before or things have got worse than they were when we started.

Contrary to how it might seem, lapses and relapses doesn't come out of nowhere. By reflecting on past patterns and learning to sit in discomfort instead of pushing it away immediately, we can learn to slow down the process of engaging in automatic behaviours and choose to turn up the volume on the internal conversation that takes place before, during and after a lapse.

That's what *The Kindness Method* tries to provide through some of the maps: reminders of everything else you have going on that you're succeeding at and have succeeded at before. Reminders of the fact that one 'slip' doesn't have to dictate who you tell yourself you are.

Reminders that you have many eggs in many baskets and that a blip needn't mean a catastrophe when it comes to personal development.

> One 'slip' doesn't have to dictate who you tell yourself you are. Remember that you have loads of eggs in loads of baskets when it comes to personal development.

About the Maps

For me, there is something very impactful about seeing a collection of reasons I have for wanting to change written down in one place, in my own handwriting. At that critical moment when I desperately want nothing more than to lapse into old ways, it would simply be impossible to bring all these reasons to the forefront of my mind. But they're all on a map. And I'm more inclined to look at them if they're written by me in a format I can just glance at (scattered around on one page as opposed to written out in lines).

It's so much harder to give up when I see that whole page of excuses and delay tactics I've already explored, pre-empted and prepared for previously. When I can see how creative (and sometimes utterly ridiculous) my excuses are when written down, I'm much less likely to try to use them again. For example, I've been known to justify abusing myself with food binges after months of staying on track because 'it's raining' or 'so-and-so annoyed me'.

Your maps will also help you to challenge complacency and 'euphoric recall' – a term commonly used when talking about drugs – to describe the tendency of people to remember past experiences in a positive light and overlook the negatives. The further we move away from all the ways our lives were impacted negatively and settle into our new 'normal', the more we are at risk of forgetting how important it was for us to change in the first place.

The good news is that once we get into the habit of noting down all the new, positive stuff we are experiencing, we realise that our lives have improved in so many small ways that we hadn't even anticipated. For example, if I'm feeling cold at someone's house and they offer me a jumper, I can accept it now. I know that may seem trivial, but there was a time when I'd stay cold – or leave – so that I wouldn't have to risk them not being able to find a jumper big enough for me. When I initially listed my reasons to lose weight, 'borrowing jumpers at people's houses' wasn't high up there on the list, along with, say, 'not being constantly out of breath'. In fact, it wasn't on the list at all. But one day it popped into my head and I realised that was something I just didn't have to think about any more. Now it's listed on my map along with the hundreds of small, surprising and wonderful ways my day-to-day life has improved. So when I look at that map in the moments when I'm romanticising old, mindless, comforting food binges, it reminds me that I have more things to lose than I can bring to the forefront of my attention (especially in moments of stress, sadness and boredom). All I have to do is make myself look at that map when I want nothing more than to fall off the wagon and then eat the wagon. Within seconds my resolve is strengthened.

When you've created your collection of maps, filled with strengths, achievements and personal insight, you can challenge those moments of euphoric recall. Some of my clients take photos of their maps and keep them on their phones to refer to in times when their resolve is challenged the most. Others have created business-card sized versions to carry in their wallets. They're a reminder of where you've been, where you want to get to and why you started in the first place.

Rather than carrying their maps with them to update when something springs to mind, some of my clients write quick notes on their phones under headings that correspond to the map headings. That way, every time they observe a moment of strength, an unhelpful thought or automatic impulse, they can capture it there and then. Some people like to keep maps and pens on a bedside table so that they can dedicate five minutes (sometimes even less) to noting them down in the morning or at night. Aside from helping them populate the maps as a useful resource, it can be a pleasant daily ritual.

A note on the maps and exercises in
The Kindness Method

The more time and consideration you give these tools, the more they will serve you. As well as the importance of the content, the long-term effectiveness of the approach relies on you being taken aback by the visual element of seeing a whole page full of words you've written in your own handwriting, powerfully reminding you why you're doing this. Before you've zoomed in to see what you've written specifically, I want the initial thought to be, 'Wow, that's a lot of reasons/ strengths/triggers.'

The maps also naturally lead on from each other. I know how tempting it is to jump to the action-planning maps and get going. Try to see it this way – overall you will get where you want to be more quickly (and stay there more easily) if you invest more time on these first maps of the process.

I recommend copying the map headings and exercises into a separate notebook, ideally one that's side-bound, so you can directly compare some of the maps side by side. You may well find some of the exercises more useful than others and want to repeat them or start creating lead-on exploratory maps of your own with new headings once the cues and suggestions in this book have got your juices flowing.

The very first time you go through completing all the exercises in this book in order, there will be more reflection time required, to bring your experiences up to present day. Unless otherwise stated, I recommend treating each chapter that contains exercises as a private session. First read the background and guidance, and then complete the exercises and reflect on what you've written. It is in keeping with the holistic spirit of *The Kindness Method* that you protect this time and commit to a process of general personal development. Acts of self-kindness like this reinforce self-worth and can help us to feel more invested in the process of change.

If possible, get into the habit of reading what you've written down on your exercises out loud. My intention is for this book is to provide you with a therapeutic experience that is private, but still benefits from the guidance of a practitioner. One of the most powerful elements of one-to-one talking therapies and support groups is hearing ourselves out loud. Not only can it take some of the power away from the thoughts and ideas we want to push out, but it helps us be more reasonable and feel more accountable. This practice can also create a useful separation that helps us notice what we're thinking in response to what we're hearing. This in turn can help us develop our self-awareness further and generate new ideas. For example, you could read your 'Ways I'm Happy to Be' map out loud in front of a mirror and listen in on the thoughts that go through your mind while you're doing it. Are you talking yourself up but thinking yourself down?

The idea is that long term you get into the habit of regularly updating maps with new experiences and anything else that has sprung to mind since you last visited them.

Finally, I encourage you to be as honest as possible, especially about the things you may not usually want to say out loud. With that in mind, it may be worth deciding how you will keep your notes private.

CHAPTER 4
SNAPSHOT LETTER

___

Most of my referrals come in on Sunday mornings. Often people will have had my contact details for a while, but a recent, unwanted incident has taken place or a situation has escalated, causing them to write asking for help. This can be anything from having behaved in a way they're not proud of the night before, to weighing themselves that morning and seeing numbers they hoped they'd never see. I also get a notable surge in referrals during the third week of January. I'm generalising here, but for the most part this is because people have got going with their resolutions but not managed to keep them up. Very often this is because they believed that the only planning required was a genuine desire to change, as opposed to a comprehensive investigation of their behaviours.

One of the ambitions I have for everyone who uses *The Kindness Method* is that their New Year's resolutions for the rest of their lives will become, 'Just carry on doing what I'm doing'.

It's always interesting to observe how much people have minimised the negative impacts of their habits by the time I see them face to face. Usually their initial email sounds pretty urgent, with statements like: 'that's it', 'something has to change', 'I'm bored of this', 'I need to accept there's an issue', 'I'm ready to do something about this'. Again, this is usually because they've contacted me as a reaction to an emotive experience. But when their bodies start feeling better, people have forgiven them for their behaviours, time has passed and they have gained a greater sense of perspective, they understandably welcome the relief of realising their reality isn't as bad as it had felt in those hopeless, helpless moments. The problem is, those moments invariably find them again.

You are presumably reading this because you've experienced those moments of exhaustion and helplessness, where you feel that your habits (or inability to start new habits) are the boss of you. Perhaps you're feeling disillusioned with miracle cures and even resentful that you're the kind of person who needs help and isn't just naturally motivated to make changes. And yet maybe as you read this, things don't seem as urgent as they did when you purchased this book in the first place.

We've talked about how quickly we can forget those moments when it's most important for us to change, so I'm going to now ask you to capture them in written form. Because as you start making changes (especially in the early stages), you are likely to fall into traps where you feel complacent or you experience euphoric recall. You may look at the number of excuses in this book and start to suspect you're making a big deal out of something that's not that serious. Maybe (like me) you wish that you already had all the maps completed so that you can just change right now without putting the work in. Either way, you will need to accept that there will be many points in this process when you want to give up. Devices like the 'Snapshot Letter' exercise you will complete at the end of this chapter will serve as a useful reminder of where you were when you started.

You don't need to be specific about what plan you want to put into action for now – I'll guide you through that later. For now, I just want you to think of 'future you', who may try to trivialise the behaviour (or absence of behaviour) that is causing you concern. This letter will become something you refer to frequently in the initial stages of your journey, especially during that dangerous window of time when you're starting to feel the discomfort of acknowledging you want to change but it's still too early to see any obvious shifts, benefits or results.

Paul's Story

Recently I was working with a client – let's call him Paul – who completed the 'Snapshot Letter' exercise during our first session. Paul was fed up, as another year had passed without him doing anything about the fact he hated his job. He was tired of complaining about it, and having just been passed up for the promotion that was meant to make sticking around a bearable prospect, he was adamant that it was time to make changes – once and for all.

He had joined the company straight after university and now, eight years later, he was still there. He wished he was working in a more creative industry as he'd always imagined he would. He had also got into a routine of going to the pub most weekdays after work to moan with other colleagues about how much they disliked the company and the other members of staff. It wasn't uncommon for him to come into work feeling tired and demotivated as a result of being hungover. This meant that he'd spend the day eating stodgy, unhealthy, comforting food, which was starting to make him feel sluggish. His whole lifestyle had started to really get him down. He admitted to me that at first he had felt quite lucky to be paid to do a job he could manage to do when hungover and it hadn't mattered to him that he wasn't challenged. But now his body was feeling the strain and he'd got to a stage where he wanted a greater sense of purpose. He missed feeling capable, productive and proud of himself. He wanted to fall into bed feeling he'd achieved something that day. The longer this pattern continued, the higher his tolerance for alcohol became, the more his self-esteem dropped and the harder he found it to believe he was capable (or worthy) of looking for or securing a better job.

When it came to addressing his habits, Paul told me his priorities went in this order:

Habit 1 to change: Putting off making the time to search and apply for new jobs.

Habit 2 to change: Drinking on weeknights.

Habit 3 to change: Eating unhealthily and not treating body well.

Ultimate goal: Getting a new job and have a healthier, more balanced lifestyle.

The initial short-term plan Paul wanted to put into place: Stop drinking altogether, go straight to the gym every night after work, then go home, eat only fruit, salad and fish and spend three hours every evening job hunting.

The short-term plan I suggested: Choose two nights in the week when you find it easiest to resist going to the pub (perhaps Monday, or nights when the people you most enjoy hanging out with aren't there). Put two hours aside during those evenings to work on your CV and scan for jobs. Identify two healthy meals you find delicious and eat those on the designated no-pub, job-hunting evenings. The mornings following these evenings (presuming you'll be feeling a bit more energetic), get off the bus two stops early on the way to work and walk the rest of the way, listening to music you really like.
(Notice how Paul's plan feels kind of like a punishment and my plan is on the kinder side.)

It's very common for people to want to do a complete overhaul, change everything at once and try to become a 'whole new person'. This is fine, but it creates quite a height to fall from if you don't manage to live up to these expectations. In the short term, it's more important to show yourself you can stick to your plan than to make huge changes.

These first stages are mainly about increasing confidence in yourself and your capabilities by pleasantly surprising yourself in as many small ways as possible. So your goals need to be as realistic and doable as possible. When you're feeling stronger, you can become more ambitious. I can't tell you how many people want to create an initial fitness plan that would be ambitious for a professional sportsperson when they've been largely sedentary for years.

In summary, the whole ethos of *The Kindness Method* is that these first stages minimise the possibility of you having mean, 'I've ruined it' conversations with yourself and increase the frequency of the 'YES, I've surprised myself again!' conversations.

Our Habits are Interconnected

In addition, and Paul is a good example of this, very often our habits are related. The great news is that often identifying the main habit you're not happy with and actively addressing it results in the other not-so-good habits also being impacted positively. By virtue of the fact that he's spent an evening eating healthily and putting wheels in motion to change jobs, Paul is likely to wake up feeling proud, capable and more energetic and rested. Not having a hangover will mean he's likely to make healthier food choices and be more tolerant about the things he doesn't like about his job and, overall, his alcohol intake will decrease.

At first Paul was absolutely delighted with the change in his routine. He knew that all his reasons for leaving his job and changing his patterns of behaviour were sound. He felt brave and empowered in a way he hadn't done in ages. His reasons to pursue a different career path remained unchanged. Plus, he was drinking far less as a result of not going to the pub with colleagues after work, as he had done for so many years. We had a couple of sessions when he would talk about how much he was enjoying going to coffee shops instead and rewriting his CV, researching jobs online that he really wanted and just taking a fresh perspective on life.

Then, about three weeks in, he came into our session looking exhausted. He told me he now felt that he'd been deluding himself. He'd received a few job rejections and missed out on a few good nights that others had reported were really fun. He was sick of making the same stir-fry over and over again. He started telling me about how much he actually loved his old job and how he'd been a bit over-dramatic coming to see me in the first place. He seemed to be remembering things very differently to how he did when he first contacted me. Suddenly, the passive-aggressive boss who he'd explained had worn him down slowly over the years was just 'misunderstood'. The monotony and lack of creativity involved in his role had become the comforting routine that he was most suited to. He was now normalising the regular drinking that he had expressed concern over by saying that he didn't drink nearly as much as some of his colleagues and actually he just simply loved booze.

I let him go on and list his reasons for not caring about changing as much as he once (quite recently) thought he did. After all, I wasn't the one who thought he was drinking too much or that his job was soul-destroying – he was. He was arguing with himself and I got the impression he wasn't very happy with me either. I knew what was going on, and from experience with both my clients and myself, I'd expected it. His confidence had taken a knock and his motivation was fluctuating. The unknown had gone from being exhilarating to terrifying. The change in status quo had gone from being novel to boring.

So I simply showed him the 'Snapshot Letter' he had written to himself immediately following our first session. He was shocked to see how upset and fed up he had been, just weeks beforehand. He was also shocked to realise how much he was omitting from his now somewhat romantic story about his workplace and the impact it was having on his drinking. We worked on accepting that there would be many more moments of uncertainty to come, and each time he remembered something he didn't like about the way things were before, he would add it to his 'Snapshot Letter'.

'Snapshot Letter' Guidance

I'd now like you to write your own Snapshot Letter in a separate notebook, using as many of the cues overleaf that resonate with you. I'm going to expect that you will go through the same stages that Paul did, so it is important to have something you can look at to remind you why you wanted to make the changes in the first place.

Copy out and use only the cues that makes sense for you. The more you write the better. Remember, while I certainly don't hope that you're in your most exasperated state right this second, that's the sort of moment we're trying to capture here. So that may mean you thinking back to those instances when the urgency and importance of making changes has felt most real. And ... Go!

Dear *(insert your name),*

It's *(insert date),* **you're** *(insert where you are while you write and what's generally going on in your life right now)*

You've decided to try this new approach because ...

- You're fed up of constantly ...
- Every Monday or New Year or summer you decide to change and you're tired of ...
- Once and for all you need to ...
- It's about time you started ...
- It's about time you stopped ...
- This is urgent and things have to change because you feel like ...
- Your opinion of yourself when it comes to being able to change is currently that you're ...
- There are some reasons that are making you want to change that you're not too proud of. It's time to be honest with yourself and admit that these include ...
- Your inability to change has brought you to a point where ...
- When you see other people managing to make changes that you can't, it makes you feel like ...
- If, over the next weeks, you're tempted to trivialise how important it is for you to change, you need to remember that ...
- Other people don't know the extent to which this has become a problem. You never thought you'd get to the stage where you're ...
- If you start finding it harder than you expected, remember it's important to push through because ...
- If you spend another year feeling like this about not making lasting changes, it will mean ...
- You need to take this seriously because ...
- Before it was okay to be like this because ... but now it's not okay because ...
- If you don't find your own way of taking control now you'll end up having to ...
- It's important to you to become more self-aware in general because ...
- You want to feel like you're ...
- You'd hoped by now that ...
- Your life is on hold and that's ...

Congratulations! You've started on your process of change and having written this letter, you've captured why this is so important to you and why it will mean more to you than ever when you get where you want to be. You already have a powerful tool to keep you on track in those moments when you want to trivialise your desire to change.

———

CHAPTER 5
WAYS I'M HAPPY
TO BE

——

One of the most important aspects of *The Kindness Method* is making a commitment to a lifelong process of feeling good about who you are. Not only does liking and accepting yourself help you to consider yourself worthy of living the life that you want, it also makes you feel just as able as anyone else to achieve your goals.

This is not about wanting everyone to live on a cloud of unconditional (and unrealistic) positivity. I think it's really important to be able to take on criticism and accept feedback about ourselves both professionally and personally. When this happens, the difference between hearing 'there's something wrong with this behaviour' and 'there's something wrong with me' is self-esteem. We're not ready to accept what we're not so great at until we are absolutely sure of what we are great at.

Acknowledging our strengths so we can be brave and open to hearing our weaknesses anchors us in a sense of who we are. It means we can listen to what others have to say about us in a fair and rational way. We can decide whether we agree with them when they give us negative feedback. When we're not confident in what we know to be undeniably good about us, we are vulnerable to taking on all feedback as though it's true – positive and negative. And we're reliant on people like our friends, partners and employers to tell us who we are and what we're good at. This reinforces the idea that other people's opinions of who we are are more important than our own, and that can hinder our ability to create plans that uniquely work for us.

Talking Ourselves Down

When I had become a more experienced training facilitator, I would commonly do a 'check-in', which required delegates to start and end the day by taking turns to say a few words about who they were or how they felt. I learned very early on that asking people to declare one single positive quality about themselves as a form of check-in was enough to make them recoil in a state of cringe. 'Hidden talents' was sometimes easier to swallow.

At first I thought this was because people (understandably) tend not to like sharing personal things in a group – not least when it's in a professional setting. But then I started to ask clients I was seeing one-on-one the same question, and the same thing would happen. Yet when I asked them to describe the positive attributes of someone they cared about, compliments rolled off their tongues so easily.

We need to accept that attempting to change this habit of not acknowledging our strengths more than our weaknesses (and indeed, changing anything we're used to doing) is going to be very hard at times. There are many other (fantastic) books available that beautifully explain neural pathways and why creating new habits is so hard. But for the sake of keeping it simple here, let's just say that when you've done something one way for a really long time, whatever that is, it's the way you're used to and comfortable with. Even if that way is not serving you any more, it's your default mode – your comfort zone, your status quo. Anything can become a habit: if you'd spent the last ten years picking flowers every day and someone asked you to stop all of a sudden, you'd be in your own version of withdrawal.

There will be moments when you don't believe in yourself or your abilities, or you seriously doubt that you possess all the positive qualities you require to be capable or worthy of changing, or of putting yourself through something difficult for long-term gain. At first, until you've found a better way of doing things, you will be swimming against a pretty strong current. In some cases this current will come in the form of physical withdrawal and discomfort. In most cases it will come in the form of sceptical and demoralising internal dialogue.

Couch Analogy

I often ask my clients to imagine their minds as a room with a couch that has someone sitting lazily across it, taking up all the space. This character has been getting more and more comfortable on the couch for a while, and really settling in. When we're tired and fed up or think we've done something wrong, it starts saying horrible things to us. It says we're weak and lazy and deluding ourselves if we think we can have ambitious goals. It tells us to stop trying and just accept that we're not as good as other people and that liking ourselves is stupid and impossible.

I then introduce a second character into the room. It's very apprehensive, shy, softly spoken. It has come into a very unwelcoming environment and really wants to sit on the couch, but it's clear that there's barely any room. Eventually, the second character goes over and manages to find a sliver of space on the arm of the couch to perch on. Slowly it allows itself to get more comfortable and eventually plucks up the courage to speak to the mean, comfortable inhabitant. In those moments when the mean character is yelling abuse, the new character starts (quietly and curiously at first) to challenge the accusations and insults. When the first character calls us stupid, the new character says, 'I hear what you're saying but actually he/she is doing all these things that show he/she is not stupid at all. In fact, it looks like he/she might actually be quite intelligent. Other people see it and he/she tries her best. Are the things you're yelling at him/her even true or are you just used to being like this now?'

Initially, the first character will always win the argument. The new one doesn't stand a chance. But slowly, as the conversation continues over time, the first character starts moving over, entertaining this new conversation and making space. Meanwhile, the new character starts getting more comfortable, and spreading out a bit. All the while, the whole room starts feeling better. The new character has turned some lights on, tidied up a bit and created a nicer atmosphere to be in. Eventually, at times when we're tired and fed up and still quick to listen to the first character, we realise that we're now listening to a curious debate, rather than an angry rant.

The 'Ways I'm Happy to Be' map you will now complete will help you to create a script for the fairer, more helpful, more truthful new character you want to be listening to.

'Ways I'm Happy to Be' Map Guidance Part 1

Starting this map marks the beginning of a lifelong live collection of your strengths and qualities you like about yourself. First, write 'Ways I'm Happy to Be' in the middle of a blank page, and draw a bubble around it. Then simply start noting down all the things you like about yourself, drawing bubbles around each one of these as you go. Try to keep your entries brief on this map – a single word or no more than a few words for each one. See the example map at the end of the chapter.

When you start writing these down, notice any caveats that pop up in your mind. For example, if you want to write 'intelligent', you may hear, 'But you're not as intelligent as ... You could have read more books on ... You may be intelligent when it comes to ... but not when it comes to ...' It's okay to hear those. It's more than okay, in fact. Hearing that stuff is key to becoming more self-aware and starting to understand what has held you back from making lasting changes in the past. You will do some exercises later that address these caveats, exceptions and conditions. For now, I just want you to write down the quality or characteristic.

Whether something is positive or not in different contexts is completely up to you. For example, you may feel that being quiet at work is a quality that you're proud of because it allows you to absorb all of the information you need to gain a proper understanding of something. Others may perceive quietness as a quality they don't like about themselves, so it wouldn't go on the map.

'Ways I'm Happy to Be' Map Guidance Part 2

This map is very much about quantity as well as quality. If every day you can observe just one thing you've handled well, or a positive quality you've demonstrated to yourself about yourself, or a meaningful compliment someone else gave you, or a way you've surprised yourself in a way you like, at the end of the year you'll have 365 of them. Then, when you start to have the kinds of mean conversations with yourself that can throw you off track or make you feel unworthy of achieving your goals, you can look at the map and challenge that internal bully on the couch. Not just by reading the words on the map but by feeling the impact of seeing an over-whelming number of positive words about yourself on one page.

With that in mind, I would like to offer you even more suggestions to help fill out your 'Ways I'm Happy to Be' map a bit more.

First, check that you've included any of the following, and if not, write them down on the map too.

- Strengths you've demonstrated at work
- Strengths you've demonstrated at home
- Strengths you've developed over time
- Positive qualities that have always been a part of who you are
- Positive qualities you've developed as a result of your upbringing
- Positive qualities that have developed over time (by accident and on purpose)
- Things you like about the kind of friend you are
- Ways you treat people that you would like to be treated yourself
- Ways you are lovable without doing anything but being yourself
- Reasons you're a good partner/sibling/parent
- Things you like about your appearance
- Things you like about how you engage with the world

'Ways I'm Happy to Be' Map Guidance Part 3

Finally ...

- Think about a person you admire and what you believe their strengths to be. Do you demonstrate any of those same qualities or abilities? If so, add them to your map
- Consider what loved ones and colleagues would consider to be your strengths and write those down too
- Refer to the list of qualities below

Suggestions:	Clever	Ethical	Insightful
Accomplished	Committed	Exciting	Intelligent
Accountable	Compassionate	Extraordinary	Intuitive
Active	Confident	Fair	Kind
Adaptable	Conscientious	Faithful	Knowledgeable
Admirable	Considerate	Fit	Laid-back
Adventurous	Courageous	Focused	Logical
Ambitious	Creative	Forgiving	Lovable
Amiable	Cultured	Friendly	Loving
Appreciative	Curious	Fun-loving	Loyal
Articulate	Daring	Funny	Mature
Astute	Decent	Generous	Methodical
Attentive	Decisive	Genuine	Meticulous
Attractive	Dedicated	Gracious	Moderate
Aware	Determined	Hardworking	Modest
Balanced	Dignified	Healthy	Nurturing
Beautiful	Disciplined	Helpful	Objective
Brave	Dynamic	Honest	Observant
Brilliant	Effective	Honourable	Open
Calm	Efficient	Humble	Optimistic
Capable	Elegant	Humorous	Organised
Captivating	Eloquent	Idealistic	Outspoken
Caring	Emotional	Imaginative	Passionate
Charismatic	Empathetic	Impressive	Patient
Charming	Energetic	Independent	Perceptive
Cheerful	Enthusiastic	Innovative	Personable

Persuasive	Realistic	Self-reliant	Successful
Playful	Reflective	Self-sufficient	Supportive
Popular	Relaxed	Sensual	Talented
Positive	Reliable	Settled	Tolerant
Powerful	Resilient	Sexy	Tough
Practical	Resourceful	Shrewd	Trusting
Precise	Respected	Skilful	Trustworthy
Principled	Responsible	Sociable	Understanding
Productive	Romantic	Sophisticated	Unique
Proud	Sceptical	Spontaneous	Vibrant
Punctual	Secure	Strong	Warm
Purposeful	Self-aware	Strong-willed	Wise
Rational	Selfless	Stylish	Witty

Congratulations! You've completed your first map of many.

'Ways I'm Happy to Be' Map: Example

This map is a sample for guidance purposes only.

Make yours personal to you, in your own handwriting.

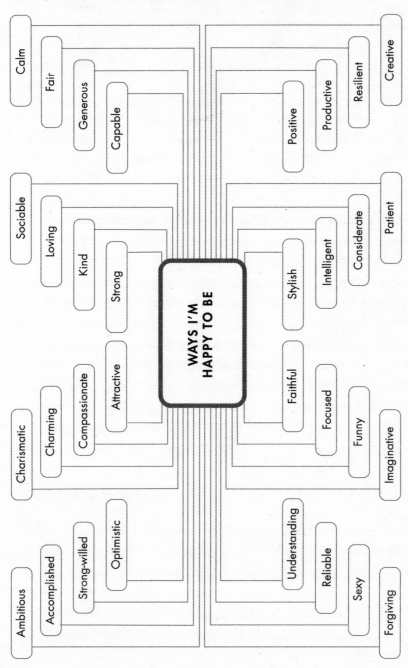

CHAPTER 6
WHAT I'M PROUD OF

Think of the last time you did something you were really proud of. Perhaps it was a big thing you celebrated with friends and got some kind of certificate or reward for. Perhaps it was something less obvious, like managing for the first time not to lose your temper with someone who really gets on your nerves. Maybe it's just that you've been meaning to be the kind of person who drinks enough water and now you do. Either way, when we manage to achieve something we feel proud of, in that moment we feel empowered and capable. The problem is, this feeling is soon forgotten. The feelings of excitement, relief and novelty wear off all too quickly and then we're on to the next goal, or we start to notice things that aren't so great about our achievement because it's presented another challenge, and so on.

Remember to Remember How Much You've Already Done

In the past, each time I reached my goal weight or finally fitted into the dress I had worked all those months to get into, I remember being ecstatic. That day nothing bad could touch me. I was friendly and positive and loving towards myself and others. I was productive and spontaneous and brave. I was so proud of myself that I felt my most resilient against temptations of bingeing on unhealthy foods or speaking to myself horribly. But only a couple of days later, I would start thinking about things like my loose skin and how I resented not being one of those people who could eat whatever they wanted. I still weighed my 'goal weight' and fitted into my 'dream size', but all it had taken was a couple of days for the high of my achievement to deflate. I was on to the next thing. After all the effort I had put in during the journey, I would spend barely any time at the destination.

The same happened with my degrees, and with jobs. Before I knew it, I'd moved on from celebrating my achievements to considering what I should be worrying about next. Don't get me wrong, there were a lot of things not to like about many of the jobs I've had, but that had nothing to do with the fact that I had achieved something I'd worked hard for and I had demonstrated I was capable.

Now I have a map full of everything I've ever been proud to have done, or managed, or survived, entitled 'What I'm Proud of'. When I feel overwhelmed and start to doubt my abilities I take a look at it. All at once, I can see all the things I have achieved over the years, and that directly and objectively challenges the doubting part of me. So the purpose of the 'What I'm Proud of' map you will complete at the end of this chapter is to help you to recall quickly the times when you've impressed yourself. Getting into the habit of adding to it can also encourage more regular practices of daily gratitude through this frequent acknowledgement of what's going right for you.

The Kindness Method is intended to help you go through as many days as possible feeling like you do when you've done something you're proud of. When you feel capable and strong, you're better placed to test and strengthen your resilience. You know that you have the ability to pleasantly surprise yourself and you're excited to keep populating your map. You can be more ambitious with your goals and feel confident in your ability to achieve them. This map also helps us not to take milestones for granted and to remember how far we've come, as our achievements become precious talismans.

Make It as Personal as You Can

Again, just as with your 'Ways I'm Happy to Be' map, when you complete the 'What I'm Proud of' map, try to note down the things that really feel like achievements to you, even if others wouldn't necessarily recognise their importance. I worked with a client once who had run the London marathon a few times. Needless to say, that's an incredible achievement and a very challenging thing to do. As such, it featured on her 'What I'm Proud of' map. But something else that featured on her map and gave her a great sense of pride was much more personal. Her father had recently been very ill and for three months she would drive for two hours in rush-hour traffic after work to the hospital to keep him company. At the same time, she and her husband were in the middle of a lot of construction work at home, and her workload had increased considerably. Eventually her father was discharged, the house was finished and her work quietened down.

When she looked back on that difficult time, she felt immensely proud of how she had handled it. She realised that a few years prior to that she probably would have dealt with the stress and sadness by lashing out at her husband and children and engaging in unhealthy behaviours. This time she had applied the new, healthier coping strategies that she'd worked hard to develop, like short breathing meditations and self-care rituals. So when it came to listing her achievements during this period, she had a lot to write.

'What I'm Proud of' Map Guidance

As with the last map, I would like you to give this one a theme, by writing 'What I'm Proud of' in the middle of a blank page, with a bubble drawn around it. Then, note down your answers to the following questions anywhere you'd like on the page, drawing bubbles around each one of them as you go. See the example map at the end of the chapter.

Tip It may be useful to refer to your 'Ways I'm Happy to Be' map to get the juices flowing, as you can review your strengths and then reflect more specifically on the particular occasions and instances when you have demonstrated them.

What have I done 'right'?

What have I accomplished?

What's felt good?

What did I pleasantly surprise myself with?

If younger me could see my life now, what would she/he be relieved/proud has happened?

What am I proud of myself for?

What have I celebrated that has to do with me?

What occasions in my life have made loved ones proud of me?

What good stuff has happened that I never thought would?

What good things have I achieved by trying?

What good things have I attracted just by being me?

What have I done that makes me feel 'capable'?

Additional Uses for a Well-populated, Up-to-date 'What I'm Proud of' Map

No More Failed Resolutions

Over the last few years I've started something of a New Year's Eve ritual and I shared it with a few of my clients. For so many years, I associated the turn of the year with feeling disappointed in myself. Disappointed that I was making the same resolutions again. Disappointed that I'd spent the last two weeks eating and drinking myself into a state where I was so bloated and tired my shoes were tight. Disappointed that I was isolating myself with food. Or, if I'd gone out, sad that everyone was having fun except me and I just couldn't wait to go home. A few years ago I decided enough was enough. Now, around New Year's Eve, I sit and reflect on my 'What I'm Proud of' map. I remember all that I withstood during testing times, things that came out of nowhere, obvious fruits of my labour and milestones across different areas of my life. It feels really great to start the New Year feeling proud, accomplished and capable.

A lot of the skills you've demonstrated in one area of your life will be transferable across many other areas. That's important to remember when it comes to applying the approaches from *The Kindness Method* over and over again for a range of unwanted behaviours as and when they crop up. The first plan you put into action will provide an opportunity to populate these maps further. But we don't yet know what you'll want more insight into in ten years' time, or what your short-term goals will be for addressing habits that have emerged or for activating difficult plans. By that point, I'd like you to have a collection of so many examples of when you showed you're more capable than you thought you were, across so many areas of your life, that it's unlikely that you haven't already, at some point, demonstrated the skills you require to see a way forward.

Tackling 'Imposter Syndrome'

Another thing that a well-populated and ever-live 'What I'm Proud of' map is great for, is challenging 'Imposter Syndrome'. I rarely come across a client who doesn't feel that they're secretly something of a fraud, and who doesn't feel like their accomplishments aren't real enough to increase their self-esteem and self-efficacy. Very often, clients who have been extremely successful in their careers will be quick to assume it was a fluke or that they were in the right place at the right time, or to minimise their achievements in some other way. Surely one of the positive outcomes from the late nights and the sacrifices and the hard work should be to feel more capable and more sure of ourselves and how worthy we are of acknowledgement?

If I had told you when you were younger that you'd have achieved what you have to date, would you have expected to have higher self-esteem and more belief in your ability to overcome challenges by now? Ask yourself, 'How would my younger self imagine me to feel about myself if he/she knew what I've managed to achieve, withstand, overcome and attract into my life?' If, like pretty much all of my clients, you noticed a difference between the answer and how you're feeling at the moment, that's certainly something to think about. In case you're tempted to beat yourself up about this in itself, please try not to. It's a useful observation and we'll be working on addressing that in good time.

'What I'm Proud of' Map: Example

This map is a sample for guidance purposes only.
Make yours personal to you, in your own handwriting.

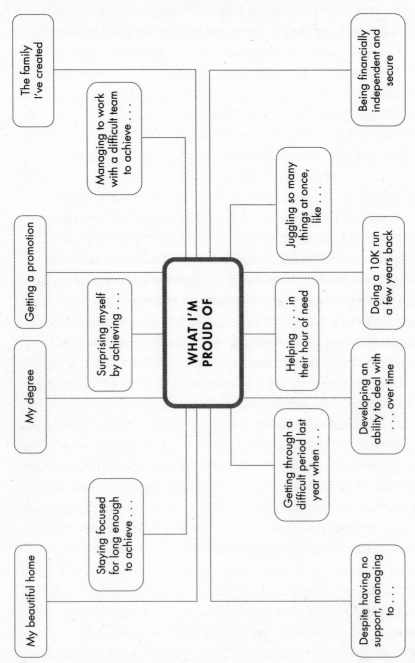

The family I've created

Being financially independent and secure

Managing to work with a difficult team to achieve . . .

Juggling so many things at once, like . . . .

Getting a promotion

Surprising myself by achieving . . .

WHAT I'M PROUD OF

Helping . . . in their hour of need

Doing a 10K run a few years back

My degree

Developing an ability to deal with . . . over time

Getting through a difficult period last year when . . . .

Staying focused for long enough to achieve . . .

My beautiful home

Despite having no support, managing to . . .

CHAPTER 7
WHEN I'M IN THE ZONE

_____

The Kindness Method is as much about cultivating self-awareness as it is about increasing self-esteem, so you can achieve the levels of resilience required to put into action and maintain your plan. The 'When I'm in the Zone' map you're going to complete in this chapter will give you an opportunity to really reflect on what makes you tick, what feels 'right' for you. It's about looking back on how you have reacted to the experiences you've had so far. Sometimes when creating a plan of change, we can make the mistake of designing it for the person we think we should be as opposed to the person we have demonstrated ourselves to be many times before.

Big shifts can take place when we start letting go of how we think and turning our focus to how we feel. When we consider what kinds of experiences make us feel good and authentically ourselves. When we think about the kinds of plans that have seemed to present the path of least resistance for us in the past. Sometimes we're not proud of what we discover about ourselves, and that's okay. Sometimes we assume that things have to look a certain way in order to work. For example, I always associated being really productive with waking up early in the morning. Turns out I can get loads done after lying in.

I've observed that the clients whose initial plans of change transpire to be most effective most quickly have something in common: they've taken time to reflect on what unique combination of elements is likely to make that plan realistic and sustainable for them personally. After all, ten people can achieve the same goal as quickly as each other ten completely different ways.

The 'When I'm in the Zone' map provides an opportunity to capture what the conditions have been like when you've successfully made things happen in the past; when you've decided to do something or change something and you've done it. This map will enable you to do a lot of the preparatory work on your own, because you are the authority on this; you are the expert.

Knowing Yourself

When I think back to the times when I've been productive and motivated, I've always had to have a routine, even if it just involves things like going to the same coffee shop for a break at the same time every day. I've also found it useful to declare what I'm doing to others (although I recognise that for some people, declaring their plans adds an element of pressure that's proven counterproductive in the past). Personally, I need quick wins, celebrations and treats to keep me going. I like to clear my diary so I don't have to worry about apologising to people if the short-term discomfort of change means I want to play my arrangements by ear. If I'm working on something on a computer, I like working late into the night. I actually enjoy the exhaustion that comes from a couple of all-nighters here and there. When it comes to doing anything very early in the morning, I've only ever been able to motivate myself for sustained periods if there's another person involved who I have to turn up for.

Think back to the times in your life when you've felt really motivated. Was it when you were doing something for someone else, perhaps? Was it when there was a strict deadline you couldn't avoid, like an exam or a holiday? Or a deadline you set yourself? Was it when you had to make changes for your health? Was it for an incentive?

Haven't I Been Here Before?

If the time you felt most motivated was when you managed to – for a while – change the habit you're now here to address, then this exercise might make you feel a bit demoralised. When I thought back to all the times I'd managed to lose weight and stick to a fitness plan, it upset me to realise how 'bad' I had let things get yet again. So, if that's the case for you, I'm genuinely sorry for the reminder. Having said that, the thing that's different is that you're going to treat these previous times when you have stalled in your efforts as part of your comprehensive planning process. You're going to increase the chances that you make a lifelong change this time by thinking about what threw you off track in the past and using lessons from each of those experiences to your advantage.

However, if you remember what made you fall off track despite periods of high motivation, don't write it on this map. Instead, make a note and save it for the map you'll be doing in the next chapter, which is specifically aimed at pinpointing the things that are likely to hinder your motivation. The 'When I'm in the Zone' map you will do now is aimed at capturing a snapshot of you when you're feeling most driven, so that you understand and can recreate those conditions the best you can when you are coming up with a realistic plan. Completing this map is an exercise in remembering that great feeling of being really driven for sustained periods of time where you're seeing results because you're feeling productive, inspired, energetic, creative, purposeful and engaged.

'When I'm in the Zone' Map Guidance Part 1

To complete the next map, you will need to reflect on some of the things you have done in the past that have required you to work hard, make sacrifices, push through difficult periods and persevere. Times when you've set your mind to something for a sustained period of time to attain a goal. Periods when you've been motivated to do something really well. When you've shown true dedication to achieving or creating something you're proud of. See the example map at the end of the chapter.

First, write 'When I'm in the Zone' in the centre of a blank page, with a bubble drawn around it. Then, write down what conditions you think enabled you to stay motivated for periods of time in the past. It may help to ask yourself any of the following questions you think are relevant:

- When was it?
- Where was I?
- What was going on at the time?
- How was I feeling in my body and mind?
- What kept me on track?
- Who was around?
- Did I get useful support from other people? If so, who? What made their support helpful? Was it their characteristics, the type of support they gave?
- Did I use any aids, like apps, journals or media? If so, what?
- How did it feel to be that motivated?
- Was there an incentive involved? If so, what was it?
- What was motivating me?
- What specifically was it about the process that suited me?
- What made it realistic for me to keep it up?

'When I'm in the Zone' Map Guidance Part 2: Reflection

Once you have completed the map, ask yourself the following questions and note down your responses either on a separate page or on the reverse side. (This can be written as normal notes, it's just to summarise any useful insights for your own reference when you come to create the best possible conditions for your next plan.)

- Do your past periods of sustained motivation seem to have anything in common? If so, what are they?
- Based on what you've written down, were you to create the perfect conditions to stick to a plan that involves changing your normal routine, what would they look like?

Reminder Go back to your 'Things I'm Proud of' map and write down what you feel you've achieved as a result of doing this exercise. Have you demonstrated any more strengths by getting this far? If so, be sure to add this to your 'Ways I'm Happy to Be' map too.

'When I'm in the Zone' Map: Example

This map is a sample for guidance purposes only.

Make yours personal to you, in your own handwriting.

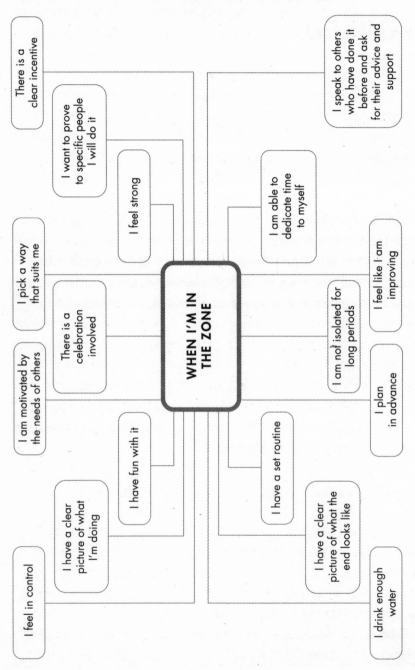

CHAPTER 8
WHAT HASN'T WORKED

___

The 'When I'm in the Zone' map you completed in the last chapter is intended to help establish what has worked for you in the past across a range of pursuits. On the next map, you will capture what definitely hasn't worked when you've attempted (or attempted to attempt) to make the change you're here to make. Perhaps you'd managed to keep up some changes for a good while before, but eventually fell off track and reverted to old, familiar ways. Perhaps something came out of the blue that derailed your plan or made it unrealistic. If you haven't ever attempted to change the habit(s) you're wanting to change now, then use the next exercise to consider any big changes you have failed to sustain in the past, despite really trying to, and what they may have had in common.

Pinpoint Where Things Went Wrong Before

So often when my clients think back to the point at which they started slipping back into old habits (which then turned into a full-blown relapse), it was something quite subtle that started off an unhelpful conversation with themselves. Sometimes it's coming back from holiday and realising six weeks later that they're still in 'holiday mode'. Sometimes it's starting to subtly grant caveats and exceptions to plans. Other times it is being tired, or the changes being so new that they genuinely forgot they were changing anything in the first place.

Identify What Doesn't Work for You

The 'What Hasn't Worked' map can help to rule out approaches that we always seem to go back to, despite them never really having worked for us. In my case, one example of this was liquid diets. Before a wedding or a holiday, I would spend money on doing one of these quickly with the intention of losing weight fast. This way, I wouldn't have to touch food, and could just live on prescribed powdered sachets that I'd just need to add water to in order to create a soup or shake. In some ways, it was the closest I could come to abstinence.

But the reality was that I simply couldn't stick to it. For years I kept signing up to these liquid diets and repeating the same pattern over and over again. I convinced myself that each time would be different. I'd think back and tell myself 'last time you didn't really want to change enough' or 'you didn't pick the right flavours'. Every time I started these plans from the beginning again I seemed to have completely forgotten all I had learned before about this approach just not being right for me. In order to keep it up for even a few days, I had to isolate myself from friends and family, staying away from social events because I was so hungry all the time and the plan did not permit me to eat anything outside of my sachets.

I had no idea how I was going to maintain my weight once I'd lost it, and I had to keep reporting to someone every week on the other side of London for a weigh-in and to purchase some more sachets containing a week's worth of liquid meals. If it was winter, you could absolutely forget that commute. Even if I'd managed to do it for a week, it could be something as basic as rain that started my internal conversation of, 'It's too horrible outside to schlep to the diet-plan representative, I'll just have one meal which won't hurt anything, then go to her tomorrow. Hmmm, what meal shall I have? Maybe every single food I've been dreaming about for the last week . . .' Cut to the following morning when I wake up, beat myself up . . .

and repeat. I always assumed that if a diet plan was proven to work for a lot of people but I couldn't manage to keep it up, it meant there was something wrong with me, not simply that it wasn't right for me.

From the perspective of wanting to keep my motivation up, I was setting myself up to fail, which meant creating a fertile ground for a mean internal conversation about how weak I was, which meant I ate more, which meant I gained more weight, which meant I signed up for liquid diets . . . you see where this is going.

Get to Know Your Patterns

When I thought back, I also noticed that if I drank even minimal amounts of alcohol while out during the evening, my resolve to stay on track with my food plan would go out of the window. I'd eat copious amounts of fast food on the way home, and the next morning, because I'd already 'ruined' the whole plan (and I was dehydrated and depleted of energy), I would have a massive greasy breakfast which would then turn into a day-long binge.

When I did the 'What Hasn't Worked' map I realised how many times post-drinking food choices had delayed my progress and each time gradually spiralled to leave me a stone heavier than I had been, before I started again a month later. So I learned to fill my fridge with things I knew I could eat without feeling like they would trigger me to relapse for days. Things that would psychologically keep me on track. Enjoyable foods I could eat freely that I didn't consider to be deviating from my plan.

'What Hasn't Worked' Map Guidance

Completing your 'What Hasn't Worked' map involves taking some time to reflect on what experience has shown simply doesn't work for you when it comes to changing the habit you'd currently like to address. It helps rule out the strategies that have proven themselves to be unsustainable for you. Some people will have one or two examples they can draw on for this exercise. Others (like me with my diets) have far more.

First, write 'What Hasn't Worked' in the centre of a blank page and draw a bubble around it. See the example map at the end of the chapter.

Ask yourself:
- What kind of plan(s) did I subscribe to?
  What elements of it weren't suited to me personally?
- What circumstances or events led up to me going off track with my plan?
- How come I didn't get back on track when things started going wrong?
- Did I stop believing in my ability to change? If so, why? What happened?
- Did I stop believing it was important to change? If so, why? What happened?

> **Reminder** Perhaps you feel more motivated now you've started to break things down like this and are taking a more in-depth, considered approach to changing this time. If so, it may be worth spending a couple of minutes now adding to your 'When I'm in the Zone' map, while any new insights into what works for you are fresh in your mind.

'What Hasn't Worked' Map: Example

This map is a sample for guidance purposes only.

Make yours personal to you, in your own handwriting.

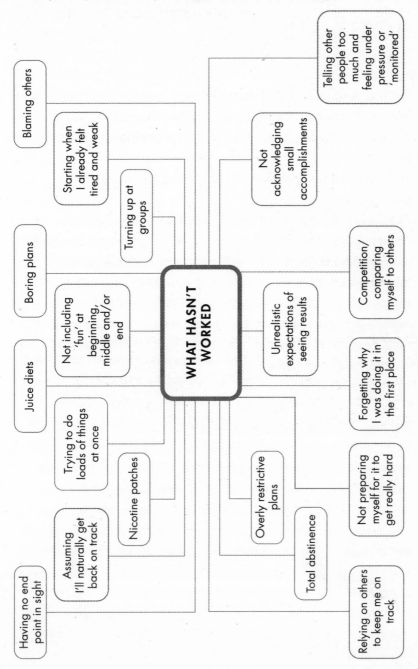

CHAPTER 9
CONVERSATIONS ABOUT ME

——

A warning about the 'Conversations About Me' map you will be completing in this chapter. I advise doing this exercise when you have the time and space to be really reflective. Consider what you'll be doing directly afterwards, because what you need to think about for this map can be a bit upsetting. This is one of those occasions where things might have to get a bit hard before they get amazing, which seems generally to be the case when we commit to the process of becoming more self-aware.

Examining the conversations we have with ourselves is one of the most important elements of *The Kindness Method*. I don't deny that there are strong internal and external forces that contribute to us not achieving our goals. However, I do believe that it's the conversations we have with ourselves, based on the assumptions we make about our own situations (and ourselves in the context of those situations) that are at the core of whether we relapse, lapse or stay on track.

Being on track in the context of *The Kindness Method* will mean that you're currently following whatever plan you've assigned for yourself. It will mean recognising when you are in active recovery, whatever that means for you. Later on in the book when you start formulating your plan, it will involve creating your own unique definitions of recovery, lapse and relapse.

When we feel our habits have gone on autopilot, the relapse process can seem to be pretty clear-cut:

We're faced with an unforeseen **High-risk Situation** *(an event, thought or feeling that tests our resolve)* that results in us lapsing from our plan.

That **Lapse** goes on to become a **Relapse** to how things were before or worse.

But when we break down the process, we can see that it's actually going like this:

Being faced with an unforeseen **High-risk Situation** + **what we tell ourselves about the situation** results in either:

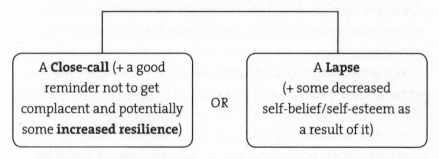

| A **Close-call** (+ a good reminder not to get complacent and potentially some **increased resilience**) | OR | A **Lapse** (+ some decreased self-belief/self-esteem as a result of it) |

If it was a **Lapse,** *not* a **Close-call**, again one of two things happens:

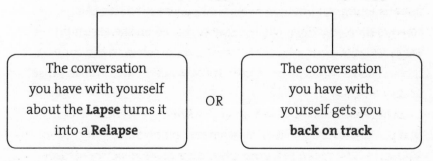

| The conversation you have with yourself about the **Lapse** turns it into a **Relapse** | OR | The conversation you have with yourself gets you **back on track** |

What's with the Self-sabotage?

A theme that runs through a lot of my conversations with clients is self-sabotage and why it happens. More often than not, once we've explored this we've found it comes down to things like low self-worth, lack of belief in their ability to truly change and/or an under-estimation of how much discomfort they can withstand in the short term.

Although self-sabotage can manifest itself through us contriving excuses to go back to our old comfort zones, it's often due to something far more fundamental. Yes, people can be seen to 'stand in their own way', especially in the early stages of change, because they want to push away the discomfort of change and the unknown as quickly as possible. As we've addressed earlier in the book, it's this mentality of avoidance that often makes us engage in the habit patterns we're here to break. But if, for a moment, we remove the element of withdrawal and short-term discomfort, why on earth would any of us want to hold ourselves back from achieving our goals and living the life we want?

In *The Kindness Method* we will look at the conversations we have with ourselves about the high-risk situations themselves and listen in on the justifications we make for going off track. While these 'excuse' conversations can be very convincing (especially when we don't articulate or write them down, a process by which we can greatly demystify them and take away a lot of their power), from my experience, addressing the conversations we have about what we're worthy and capable of can be far more powerful in ensuring that we stay on track, especially in those moments when we find it most difficult.

Investigating Yourself with Curiosity

Let's investigate the conversations that could be holding us back with an air of curiosity, and then ask ourselves when these started and what makes them so believable (other than the fact it's just the way things have been for so long). I use the words investigation, observation and curiosity a lot in my work. This is because it's so important not to see this process as a punitive one, where you start beating yourself up about how long you've been beating yourself up. Yes, when we commit to shining a light on habits that have emerged we sometimes discover things we don't like. Perhaps it's the realisation of how long we've waited to make changes, or the fact that things have got to the stage that they have. But dwelling too much on that can be completely counterproductive. So often my clients will tell me that they binged on food or drugs in reaction to having a moment of realisation about how bad things had got around food or drugs.

> *It's so important not to see this process as a punitive one, where you start beating yourself up about how long you've been beating yourself up.*

I often tell clients to imagine they are observing themselves from afar, or watching a film of their lives where they can hear their thoughts loudly as well as see their behaviours. Without judgement (or being able to feel the feelings associated with these observations), I ask that they take in what's going on with curiosity. To take an example from my own experience of going on holiday and trying to stay in my version of recovery by sticking to an eating plan, I might listen in and think:

'Isn't it interesting how, when Shahroo got on the plane, she was feeling really motivated and ready to go on holiday. She was going to stick to her plan for healthy eating and staying active. But then, when she realised she'd got so big the tray table was resting on her belly, her thoughts started saying, "This is pointless, I can't believe how weak I've been to let myself get to this size. Who am I kidding, thinking I can stick to this plan?

I've never been able to before and, let's face it, it's not like I look good as it is. And even if I did manage to get to a point where I like how I look (which is unlikely because I'm not one of those motivated people), then it'll be ages until I can walk around with confidence. Plus, this was an unrealistic plan. No one diets on holiday. I'll sort it out when I get back."

'Then she starts eating loads on the plane. Eating all the things she hasn't been eating the past few days. Then she chooses sad films to watch and spends most of the flight crying. When she gets to the airport on the other side she eats something again and her thoughts are on overdrive now, "You shouldn't have done that, you have no self-control, why can't you be one of those people who stops when they're full? Seriously, get a grip!"

'The whole holiday she carries on like this, being mean to herself. I've also noticed she doesn't seem to be wearing any of the nicer clothes she brought, or going for walks like she said she would. She keeps doing things to distract herself, like constantly checking her phone. It's really interesting how the tray-table thing turned into her coming back dragging her feet, nearly a stone heavier and with a really loud voice telling her some horrible things about herself.'

By treating habit change as a study of yourself as a human who has just developed ways of coping that have emerged over what is often a lifetime, you can start removing some of the meanness you show yourself, and make the whole process a little bit more academic and less personal. When you get used to observing things this way, it also becomes very clear how quickly a negative experience can begin a domino effect of self-sabotage. To use the example above, if I was observing myself using *The Kindness Method* (both observer-me and actual-me), perhaps it would go something like this:

'Oh no, it looks like that tray table isn't going down. She did suspect that might be the case. That can't be very nice for her considering how hard she's been trying to change her behaviour around food. The voice in her head is saying, "You knew there were going to be things that tested you and this is one of them. Remember that you wrote on your map that *experiences that made you feel you had a really long way to go would be high-risk situations for you. This is a challenge you can absolutely overcome. You have achieved so many things in the past! Plus, you deserve to get what you want and feel comfortable. This plane ride is going to be difficult but think about how you'll feel when you land, knowing you managed not to binge on unhealthy things. What can you do to be nice to yourself other than fill in some maps? Maybe watch something funny. When you feel good you make good decisions and right now you don't feel great, which is understandable! The next few hours will pass just as quickly whether you do or don't go off track with your plan. One week from now, how will you wish this had gone? What's the kind thing to do? It's going to be hard but you can do this. It was always going to be hard. But you have a choice, make the kind one. Plane tables don't get to dictate whether you have a good holiday.'*

You can see here how changing the conversation you have, realising that forewarned is forearmed when it comes to self-awareness, and taking a kind, curious approach can get you where you want to be (practically speaking) far more quickly.

These conversations become even more important when we are trying to ensure that a lapse doesn't become a relapse. It's the messages you give yourself that determine whether or not this will happen. The difference between thinking: 'I've messed up, I'm weak, I'm giving up!' and 'Useful learning, just a blip, I'm already back on track,' is kindness.

'Conversations About Me' Map Guidance Part 1

To complete this map, first write 'Conversations About Me' in the middle of a blank page with a bubble around it. Then, I'd like you to write down what kinds of things you say to yourself when you haven't managed to do something you said you would. Draw a bubble around each one as you go. See the example map at the end of the chapter.

This map is meant to be a collection of messages you give yourself when you're feeling weak and disappointed, when you've behaved in ways that you've either immediately or later regretted. Times when you're finding things harder than you think you should. A collection of the things you tend to say to yourself – about yourself – when you fall off track with a plan or think you've let yourself down in some way.

Here are some cues to get you going, based on common conversations I used to have with myself, and clients regularly tell me they have with themselves. Before you go to use them though, note down things that immediately come to mind. Each of us will have some specific beliefs and assumptions about ourselves that have developed as a result of our unique experiences:

- 'Of course I couldn't stick to the plan, it's because I'm ...'
- 'People like me don't make big changes, we're too ...'
- 'I'm just the kind of person that ...'
- 'Even if I managed it, I'd never match up to ...'
- 'The qualities that make me different to everyone else and less worthy of getting what I want are ...'
- 'Some people are naturally motivated but I'm ...'

'Conversations About Me' Map Guidance
Part 2: Observation Notes

Now read over the things you say to yourself when you've fallen off track. This is a map that is particularly impactful if you read it out loud (just the once though!).

Consider the tone in which they're said. Look at them all written down in one place and take a moment or two to think about how it comes across. Imagine all these things being shouted at you by someone else. In the event of a lapse, would the contents of this map fill you with energy, hope, confidence and the belief you need to get back up and back on track as quickly as possible? For each word or statement, ask yourself:

- When did I start thinking this was true?
- Did someone tell me this statement is true of me?
- I wasn't born thinking this about myself, so where did it come from?

If you remember that someone told you this was true of you, think about who it was. Perhaps a teacher, a parent, a partner, a friend, a sibling?

If your responses to these questions lead you to realisations about yourself that hadn't occurred to you before, acknowledge this by making a note of your new insights, either on the reverse side of your 'Conversations with Myself' map or on a separate page.

Taking Old Voices Out of New Conversations

If someone else told you that any of the negative words or statements you have written down was true of you, reflect on the circumstances in which it was said and think about how relevant it is to your life at the moment. Was the source of this information about yourself someone you think should currently be dictating whether you achieve your goals or not? Do they have the same values as you do? Is their opinion as important as the opinions of those who would challenge their insulting labels? Is their opinion important enough to hold you back from achieving what you desire and deserve?

I worked with a client recently who kept making sweeping statements about himself that often completely contradicted what I knew to be true about him. He would say things like, 'I have to do favours for people and shower them with gifts, otherwise they won't like me.' When I gently challenged this assumption and questioned it, he eventually discovered that this was a core belief he had been carrying around from very early childhood, when he had found it hard to make friends at school. This man was now in his early forties. He was surrounded with friends and colleagues who had demonstrated repeatedly that they weren't sticking around because of favours or gifts. If anything, they often told him he was doing an unnecessary amount for others and should value himself more. They weren't measuring his value on gestures. So why, three decades on, was he still working on this assumption?

Very often, we internalise something someone said to us a long time ago and simply never pause to challenge it. Professionally, we often don't seem to find it as difficult to accept we've made changes. For example: 'Five years ago I didn't have effective management skills, yet today I manage a team of fifteen people and now I would consider myself a good manager.' I've noticed that when it comes to acknowledging positive change, it's easier for clients to frame that change in terms of things they can do now, as opposed to who they are now.

Let's consider for a moment that some of the statements on the 'Conversations About Me' map were once true of you. For example, maybe as a child you picked up lots of new hobbies and never really stuck to one. First of all, why is this so bad? Why have you decided this means you're 'flakey', as opposed to someone who bravely tries out new things and knows when something isn't right for you?

Now, ask yourself, even if it was once true, is it still true now? To use the example above, I imagine that in adult life you'll have demonstrated times when you set your mind to something and achieved it, so take some time to challenge this assumption, using the 'characters on the couch' analogy I described before, along with your 'Ways I'm Happy to Be' map and 'What I'm Proud of' map. (If the example of assuming you're someone who starts things but doesn't finish them resonates with you, it may also be worth asking yourself whether it's become a self-fulfilling prophecy.)

So, what if you really do believe some of these conversations that take place contain elements that were – and are still – true, and you're not happy with them? There's a kinder way to address this too, which is the same way *The Kindness Method* approaches habits: with curiosity, acceptance and a plan to make changes that align with your values.

Accept that these assumptions will stay around for a while. In fact some people, in the short term, may hear some new, inner cruel messages, because now there's the possibility to add, 'You're so weak-willed you've had to buy a book to help you change', or 'This kindness stuff might work for some people but not me, because I'm ...' and the like. I ask that you listen in and consider challenging these assumptions with curious questions about where they came from and whether they're true (and even if they are, whether they're actually so bad). Not only is avoiding these thoughts entirely unrealistic after a lifetime of thinking one way, but trying to push them out instead of inspect them only reinforces an attitude of avoidance and fear of what's going on for us. We won't ever be made up entirely of positive qualities. The idea here is to see if we can't commit to making the ratios and conversations more fair and balanced for the rest of our lives.

Often, when we start becoming more aware of these negative thoughts and assumptions about ourselves, we don't only notice the content of them but also how frequently we repeat the same cruel things.

The Paperclip Challenge

One of the nurses I once trained shared a tip that helped a lot of her patients (and now a lot of my clients). These people had struggled to change the conversations they were having about themselves, so she asked them to start each day with thirty or so paperclips in one of their pockets. Then each time they caught themselves saying something cruel to themselves, they were to transfer a paperclip from one pocket to the other. At the end of the day they would empty out their pockets and realise how frequently it was happening. The shock of this, combined with the knowledge of how counterproductive it was, was often enough to decrease the number of paperclips they would have in the second pocket at the end of the next day. I've since used this exercise with my clients, many of whom have found it really useful. Some now have jars dotted around their homes that they throw a button or marble into every time they hear themselves saying something cruel to themselves, as a potent visual reminder of how ingrained this habit has become.

Note We all carry around core beliefs. However, some can come from childhood experiences that are very traumatic and need a more focused, perhaps face-to-face therapeutic approach. A small number of my clients have known for a while that they could benefit from some one-to-one counselling, but have been avoiding it, normalising the challenges they want to address. In those cases, *The Kindness Method* is useful in helping to explore why they are avoiding this work. We write 'to research and attend counselling' into their plan of action and pre-empt the high-risk situations for them to fall off track with this plan, as we would with any goal. Again, *The Kindness Method* is not the plan itself, but rather the guidance required to create, action and sustain a realistic plan.

'Conversations About Me' Map: Example

This map is a sample for guidance purposes only.
Make yours personal to you, in your own handwriting.

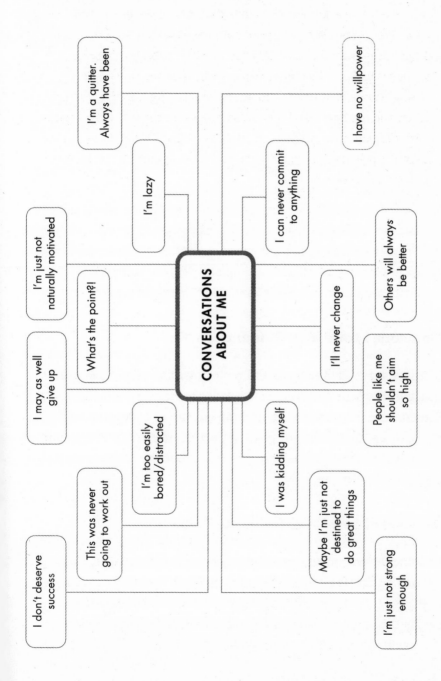

CHAPTER 10
SOMEONE I LOVE

For a lot of my clients, this exercise really brings home why it is that they haven't managed to make changes that last. In previous chapters, we've explored how important it is to speak to ourselves more kindly, which in turn impacts our behaviour and dictates how much resilience we can demonstrate in those moments of weakness.

'Someone I Love' Map Guidance Part 1

In this chapter, I'd like you first to write down the name of someone you love dearly in the centre of the page and draw a bubble around it. Someone for whom you wish nothing but success. Someone who you feel deserves to achieve any goal they set themselves. (It's important that you do write their name down clearly.) See the example map at the end of the chapter.

'Someone I Love' Map Guidance Part 2

Imagine the person whose name you've written down is trying to do something that is really challenging for them. They want to achieve their goal more than anything. They're absolutely convinced that seeing their plan through would improve their lives immensely. You know that it's quite an undertaking that will take time and perseverance. They're not sure they can succeed, plus they've tried before and not quite managed to stick with their plan and achieve their ultimate goals. They've come to you feeling disillusioned, exhausted and completely lacking self-belief. They really want to throw in the towel but despite feeling hopeless, they're really upset at the prospect of not changing things.

Around the name in the centre of your page, write down as many things you can think of to say to this person that might help them stay on track and believe that they can achieve their goal. Draw a bubble around each statement as you go.

Note down:
1   What you would tell them about themselves and what they're capable of
2   What kinds of messages or advice you think would be most helpful to them

'Someone I Love' Map Reflection

Look at the map you've created. Presumably what you have in front of you is a collection of ways to motivate pretty much anyone. Now look at your 'Conversations About Me' map, and compare the two side by side. Notice the difference. If your 'Someone I Love' map is full of the positive, uplifting, inspirational messages that you know keep people on track, is it any wonder you've struggled to make changes if all your internal conversations have been coming from the negative messages on the first map?

So What Now?

For starters, as well as reminding yourself of your strengths and achievements, you now have an additional way to challenge any mean messages you're giving yourself: reminding yourself, 'I wouldn't speak to someone else like this'.

You can start addressing this unfair dialogue by becoming aware of it when you do something you wish you'd done differently. For instance, you've locked the keys in your car or said something you shouldn't have said by accident. Instead of indulging in hours of beating yourself up with harsh internal dialogue, think about how you would respond if a friend told you that they had done something similar. Imagine if they called and said, 'My brother is really angry and upset that I won't be going to his wedding. I can't shake this feeling of guilt and worry, but I know it's the right decision for me not to go. It's really upsetting me.' Would you respond to them by saying, 'You should be worried all day. He's probably never going to speak to you again. Maybe you should go back on your decision. At the very least it's a terrible enough crime for the guilt to dominate your day.'

Presumably you'd say something more like, 'It makes sense that he's upset, but you know you did the right thing for you. Give yourself a break.'

Again, this works even better if you say to yourself out loud the advice you'd give to a friend. For many of us, it's quite shocking to hear how different (and how much nicer) we are in our external relationships than we are to ourselves in our internal monologues.

For many of my clients, profound changes start to take place with the realisation that they are not treating themselves with anything near the compassion, generosity and understanding that they show others. Please allow this process to help you make that shift and, although I know it can be extremely difficult, please try to challenge any suspicion that you're less deserving than others, or that for some reason you're the exception.

Doing It for Someone Else

Putting yourself in the place of a loved one can also be a useful tool when dealing with cravings or temptations to behave in a way you know you'll regret later. One of my clients was motivated to stop smoking following the arrival of his first child. I asked him to try spending one day treating his body how he would want his child to treat theirs. Although this may sound quite simple, I have seen countless clients push through nicotine withdrawal for 'one more day', absolutely reluctant to smoke with this idea at the forefront of their mind. In the meantime, of course, their physical withdrawal decreases and they feel more empowered as their behaviour aligns with their values. They did what they said they were going to do and they've pleasantly surprised themselves with time to protect under their belt. Admittedly this exercise is something of a 'cheat' because we're of course working towards eventually being able to like ourselves enough to care about our own wellbeing before – or at least as much as – that of others. Plus, scaring yourself out of smoking with a distressing visual is not in keeping with the spirit of *The Kindness Method* long term. But practically speaking, we want to get going and see tangible results as quickly as possible. We need to get through those initial uncomfortable stages of adjustment and come out the other side feeling accomplished and capable and resilient. At the beginning of a change process it's a case of 'whatever does the job', especially when it comes to riding through short-term cravings.

'Conversations About Me' Map: Example

Example of directly comparing 'Conversations About Me' and 'Someone I Love' maps for full impact.

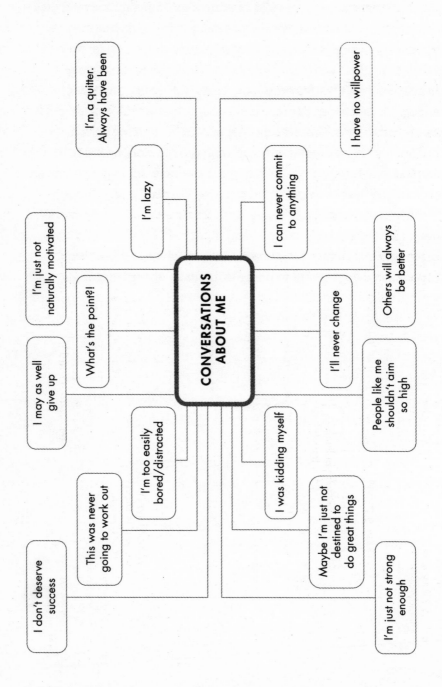

'Someone I Love' Map: Example

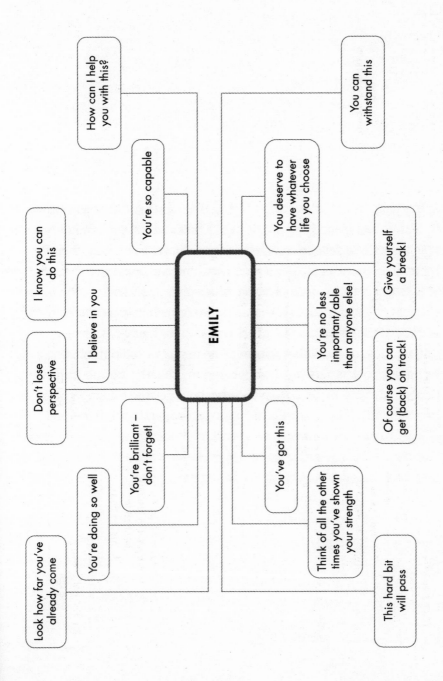

EMILY

How can I help you with this?

You can withstand this

You're so capable

You deserve to have whatever life you choose

I know you can do this

Give yourself a break!

I believe in you

You're no less important/able than anyone else!

Don't lose perspective

Of course you can get (back) on track!

You're brilliant – don't forget!

You've got this

You're doing so well

Think of all the other times you've shown your strength

Look how far you've already come

This hard bit will pass

CHAPTER 11
WHAT'S THE HARM?

———

In this chapter you will start clarifying the main habit that you want to change and identifying all the habits that surround it. Later on, you will break these desired changes into specific goals. For now, though, try to finish some or all of the sentences opposite, copying them into your own notebook, depending on which ones apply most to the main changes you want to make. Bear in mind that when you come back to use *The Kindness Method* for other plans throughout your life, different responses will be relevant. The first plan you put into action using this book is very much about learning the process and starting to populate your maps. So don't worry about getting things 'right' or overthinking this part. Just write whatever comes to mind. You can always go back and change or add to it as you remember new things. You can add as many different kinds of changes as you like here, and include as many areas of your life as you like.

> **Your Changes in a Nutshell:**
>
> I want to do more . . .
>
> I want to do less . . . I want to be more . . .
>
> I want to be less . . .
>
> I want to feel more in control of . . .
>
> I want to start . . .
>
> I want to stop . . .
>
> **The Changes I Want to Make in One Concise Sentence . . .**

What Don't You Like About the Status Quo?

At the end of this chapter you will complete a 'What's the Harm?' map to help you explore all of the negative aspects of your habits so far. It considers the ways that your behaviour and patterns have made life more difficult for you and for those around you up until now (and probably how they continue to do so currently). It is a collection of all the things that you don't like about the impact that not having made changes is having (or has had) on your life. All the negative experiences that stand out as a direct result of your doing or not doing the thing you're here to address go on this map.

Clients often assume that this map will come earlier in the process. After all, we often assume that focusing on the bad stuff will make us change. But as I mentioned earlier in the book, I learned from working in addiction that when initial meetings focus on what's wrong with people and their habits, they can disengage with the process before they've had a chance to build the confidence they will need to see this negative stuff as useful information for their recovery. Nonetheless, it is important to acknowledge why we want to change in the first place and assume that, at least on balance, the negatives are outweighing the positives.

Most of my clients have reached a stage where, in one way or another, on balance, it's more difficult to stay the same than to change. But, as with anything to do with human behaviour, it's not as simple as that. In some moments we feel that changing the way we act is the most important thing we can imagine, yet often, sometimes literally seconds later, we've gone off track and we can't think of two reasons why it's worth the effort, let alone ten or twenty. That's the beauty of your maps.

The Knock-on Effects

I recently worked with a client who was concerned about her recreational use of cocaine most Saturday nights. Through our conversations, it became clear that it wasn't buying illegal drugs that bothered her, or the cost, or her health, or indeed her behaviour while under the influence. Although these were considerations, if she was perfectly honest, the desire to get rid of these impacts wasn't strong enough to make her change for a sustained period of time. Plus, the process of buying and doing the drug itself was still really enjoyable as an isolated activity. What was bothering her most (and most strongly motivating her to change) were the periods of anxiety, self-doubt and sugar cravings that the all-nighters left her with – sometimes for many days later.

We looked at some of her patterns and realised that especially during the first half of the working week there would be a spike in her compulsive checking of her smartphone, when she would be inclined to compare herself to others on social media, ruminate over unanswered text messages, worry needlessly that her friends were upset with her, make contact with people from her past with whom she'd had toxic relationships and generally doubt herself in a way that was impacting the quality of her life.

When she was eventually no longer feeling the anxiety itself, she was left with friendships to repair, ex-boyfriends to deal with, sleep deprivation and a whole load of general self-loathing for having 'overreacted'. Even after she'd physically recovered and was in a more stable place, the judgemental conversations she had with herself about the week itself were exhausting her emotionally. Being in that mindset was something she wanted to push away as quickly as possible. So guess what her physical recovery, coupled with a need for emotional avoidance, left her wanting to do the next Saturday night? And so the cycle would continue.

This is also an example of how important it is for us not to push our values and agendas onto anyone else. If it's more important for you to stop buying cocaine because three days later it throws you into an existential crisis than it is because it's illegal, then that's what you focus on. The outcome is the same and changing your habits for your own reasons gets you there more quickly.

Once the patterns and interplays of the impact of this client's behaviour became so clear, she stopped being able to ignore how predictable her cycle was. Then we created a realistic plan for her to try. She cut down and eventually stopped using recreational drugs altogether. Not because she didn't like them any more or because she'd stopped enjoying the all-nighters, but rather because whenever she did experience this euphoric recall, she would look at the maps she had filled out in her lowest moments. She would read over the letters she had written to herself, reminding her of all the reasons why the pattern needed to stop. She would tell herself that in certain moments she was likely to feel a strong urge to go off plan, but that it was important to consider life three days after making the decision to lapse. She would make a concerted effort to remind herself of how many areas of her life were being impacted negatively. She would also look at her 'What I'm Proud of' map, which now included being able to stop using cocaine and reaching goals she never thought she would. This in turn increased her self-esteem and meant that she spoke more kindly to herself.

In this case, she also cut down how much she was drinking, as she knew that the likelihood of arranging to buy drugs would increase as her resolve decreased after a certain number of drinks. Again, it's all about self-knowledge and self-enquiry. When we get honest about our patterns, and accept them as they are, we can start making changes from an informed, empowered place, driven by our valued outcomes. When completing the next map, consider this client example and think about any interplay between your habits and how they may be impacting each other. You may discover new motivations to change that you'd never considered.

'What's the Harm?' Map Guidance Part 1

To complete this map, I'd like you to first write 'What's the Harm?' in the middle of a blank page and draw a bubble around it. Then, start to note down all the negative impacts you can think of that your current unwanted habit (or absence of desired habits) is having on your life. It may be useful to look back at your 'Snapshot Letter' exercise to get you started. Consider as many areas of your life as possible. Perhaps your habits negatively impact your family, career, health, romantic relationships, friendships, personal development, life ambitions, spirituality, social life, confidence or quality of life. See the example map at the end of the chapter.

'What's the Harm?' Map Guidance Part 2

Once you have populated your map with the negative impacts, work through and rate out of ten how important each of these things is to you, with ten being really important and one being not very important. It's vital here to really consider what matters to you personally, not what you think *should* be most important.

> **Reminder** If filling out this map has reminded you of the times you've tried and not succeeded in changing before, or the process has drawn your attention to some less-than-kind messages you give yourself about your negative behaviour, make a note of these on your 'What Hasn't Worked' and/or 'Conversations About Me' maps.

'What's the Harm?' Map: Example

This map is a sample for guidance purposes only.
Make yours personal to you, in your own handwriting.

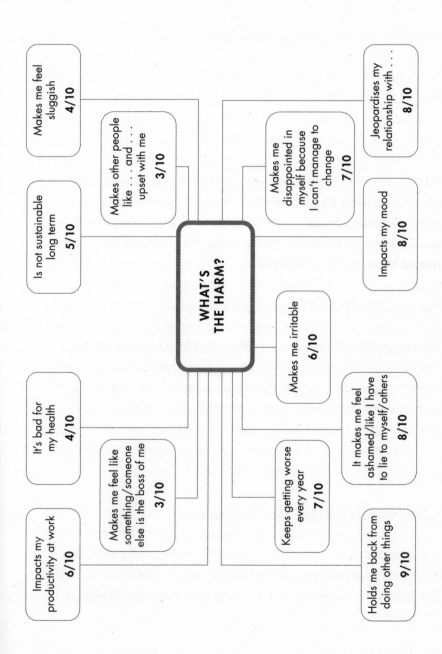

CHAPTER 12
WHY HAVEN'T I CHANGED ALREADY?

_____

The unwanted habits you've developed are not just the problem; they are, or once were, also the solution. Very often when we really want to change, we can't imagine that there are any positive aspects of the habits we so dislike. But it's really important to acknowledge what purpose these habits have been serving, not only to give us valuable insight into what new habits we want to adopt, but also to help reinforce the idea of being kind to ourselves. In this way, we realise we're not simply weak, but rather humans who have adopted habits that do (or did) serve a purpose. It's up to us to decide at different junctures in life whether the last lot of habits we've picked up still serve us, on balance, according to our values. If they don't, we can make a concerted and conscious effort to address that.

This chapter contains a map and an additional exercise. If you can, complete them all in one sitting. If not, try to work through this chapter within a couple of days if possible.

Being 'On the Fence' About Change

It's important to uncover and accept the reasons we have to stay the same, as well as our reasons to change. It's about asking: 'Why am I on the fence about change? Why isn't making this change a no-brainer?'

Often our reasons to *change* unwanted behaviours are the same as those of other people: improved health, better quality of relationships, increased self-confidence and so on. But our reasons to *stay the same* can be more personal and much less obvious – even to ourselves. By uncovering our reasons to stay the same, we can be more considered when we try to change the status quo. By knowing the extent of the comfort and habit we are taking away, we can get an idea of what we need to put in its place.

There are three questions to consider when exploring why we continue to do things that we don't want to be doing:

1 Did it once do a job that doesn't need doing any more?

I've often heard people say the following: 'I started drinking to be comfortable with …, and once I was comfortable with it, I just carried on drinking.'

If this is the case for you, then it is actually a really good place to be starting from. My clients who are in this position are often delighted to discover that they have already addressed the issue that made them take up the behaviour in the first place. Sometimes it's having been through something obvious like counselling, other times through becoming more mature and confident simply as a result of getting older and overcoming difficult life experiences. They just haven't taken time to realise the habit isn't useful or required any more but still has a hold on them nonetheless, because it's, well, a habit!

In this situation, they are usually on autopilot, and they haven't challenged the status quo in a long time. This is very often the case with alcohol, where clients assume they need to have a drink or two to give them what they perceive as confidence to deal with something like smalltalk at a work event or to initiate contact with someone they're sexually attracted to in a social context (or indeed to have sex). It isn't until maps and conversations bring to their attention how often they've demonstrated they can do comparable (and often more challenging) things when they are sober, that they realise the drinking is just a leftover habit they need to break in a practical sense and stop operating on autopilot.

One of my clients likened this realisation to taking antibiotics for a chest infection and then continuing to take them (in higher doses!) after the infection has disappeared. In that case, there would be a medical professional to draw our attention to the fact that it's time to stop. In the case of excessive and mindless consumption, many people are simply not periodically stopping to reflect on whether they still need to feel the effects they're getting from their habits.

2   Has it become less effective at doing a job that still needs doing?
I've often seen this happen with regular skunk smokers who approached community substance-misuse services when they wanted to quit. They would report that for many years the drug had worked very well in helping them relax, giving them a greater sense of perspective and making boredom an enjoyable experience. However, as their tolerance increased over time, the drug became less effective at doing these things. In fact, for some it would go the other way, and start contributing to anxious-thinking patterns.

Regardless of why the drug wasn't working as well for them any more, clients tended to have one thing in common: they had never developed alternative ways to relax, unwind and achieve the states they once relied on the drug to provide them with.

3   Is it still doing the job?
If the habit you're engaging in poses no current issues for you, then obviously continue. It may seem natural to presume that someone who was completely happy with their current habits and coping strategies wouldn't benefit from a book like this. However, even in these cases it is worth thinking about how many other strategies for coping you have in place.

So, if the habit you're engaging in still does the job really well, but you want to stop engaging in it or create new habits around it (either now or eventually), it's worth thinking about what you can add that could serve a similar purpose. Be aware that the likelihood is that the new strategy may not do the job as well, at least to begin with. But I've seen it prove very effective in these cases to approach the process by adding new things rather than taking old ones away, in the first instance. The ideal is that as the new things become more effective through practice and become habits in themselves, so the number of times you turn to the less favourable habits will gradually decrease.

Gaining true insight into why you are engaging in an unwanted habit and how to change it involves looking at how it's serving you as well as what you don't like about it. This way you can take a more compassionate and less punitive approach to uncovering what your needs are.

For example, if you use alcohol to ease social anxiety, perhaps it's time to reflect on your strengths, work on your self-esteem and challenge any negative internal dialogue left over from teenage years. If shopping helps you feel less bored, perhaps it's time to consider working on short-term distraction and tolerance skills before taking time to reignite old passions and explore new hobbies.

'Why Haven't I Changed Already' Map Guidance Part 1

I would like you to now consider the forces at play that may be making it difficult for you to let go of your status quo.

To create the next map I'd like you to first write 'Why Haven't I Changed Already?' in the middle of a blank page, and draw a bubble around it. See the map example at the end of the chapter.

Now read through the suggested possible answers over the page. When you see one that resonates with you, copy it out wherever you like and finish the sentence. Then draw a bubble around each entry as you go.

'Why Haven't I Changed Already' Map Guidance Part 2

When you feel you have finished the map for now, go back through it and rate how important these reasons feel to you out of ten, as you did with the 'What's the Harm?' map.

Staying the same

- Gives me comfort by ...
- Enables me to do things I want to do, like ...
- Helps me avoid/put off situations I don't like, such as ...
- Helps me avoid thoughts I don't like around ...
- Helps me calm down and switch off at times like when ...
- Makes me feel safe, by ...
- Helps me protect myself from ...
- Makes parts of my life easier to cope with, like ...
- Makes me feel more control of things like ...
- Gives me the confidence to ...
- Gives me a way to celebrate/commiserate ...
- Helps me punctuate achievements ...
- Makes me feel included with people and groups such as ...
- Makes things like ... less boring and more enjoyable
- Helps me put off things I don't want to/don't think I can do, like ...
- Is familiar and the only way I've known because ...
- Helps me to 'deal' with certain people like ...
- Is better than the alternative, which would be ...
- Doesn't risk changing any of my relationships negatively, such as those with ...
- Means I don't have to deal with discomfort, which I'm scared would feel like ...

'Why Haven't I Changed Already' Map Guidance Part 3

Now compare your 'What's the Harm?' map with your 'Why Haven't I Changed Already?' map. You may notice that there are far more reasons to change than to stay the same. However, if, for example, you have ten reasons to change that rate as a five out of ten in terms of importance to you and one reason to stay the same which is a ten out of ten in terms of importance, that may shine a light on why you're finding the change difficult and help you acknowledge the profound value that this habit has to you, whether you want it to or not.

> **To reiterate** *The Kindness Method* is by no means a replacement for counselling. If, by exploring what you may be trying to avoid, you uncover something that you suspect you need to take a deeper approach to working through, then I strongly advise including this kind of support as an important element of your change plan.

Developing New Strategies

We're now going to do an exercise that further explores the key insights from your collection of reasons why staying the same might be serving you. Have a look at your 'Why Haven't I Changed Already?' map. If you've realised that the only reason you're engaging in your unwanted habits is leftover learned behaviour that you don't need any more, you can write things like 'maintaining the status quo', 'the only way I know' or 'I don't really see how things can be different'. Whatever feels most right for you. Copy out and finish the sentences below in your notebook, filling in the blanks:

I now realise the reason I've stayed the same is because it's fulfilling the following needs to do so . . .
In my ideal world, I would be doing . . . instead of (or as well as) my current habits to fulfil these needs.
In the short term I could distract myself from the discomfort of not having this need met as quickly as I'm used to by . . .

It's Time to Forgive Yourself

Now, ask yourself:

- Is it now clearer to me why it's been hard to make changes in the past?
- Am I feeling less in the dark about why I am the way I am right now?
- If I've been cruel to myself for developing the habits I have, would I blame someone else for getting to this stage, considering how they have served me?

This stage in the process is highly personal but it is very important in helping you to make sure this time will be different and these changes will last. So often when we create plans, we underestimate all the forces pulling us to stay the same. When our habits are more obviously unhealthy or negative, we blame ourselves for becoming dependent on them by labelling ourselves as weak-willed. These exercises should help us to create a more forgiving dialogue with ourselves. Furthermore, by this stage it should be more apparent that the maps are a portal through which we can develop new ways of thinking, and a way to consider things we perhaps hadn't given enough attention to before. More often than not, writing these things down (especially if they're new realisations) will start us on a line of enquiry that sticks in our minds long after we've completed the exercises.

Soon you will be reaching the stage of formulating a plan with practical goals. The emotional challenges you have faced so far through doing all this self-awareness work will be compounded with practical ones which will impact your day-to-day life, your social habits, even perhaps your physical comfort. All of the preparation you've done will really be put to the test, and the need to be kind to yourself will be extremely important.

Embarking on this process doesn't just mark a commitment to planning well, making practical changes and achieving goals, it marks a lifelong commitment to being more kind, compassionate and understanding in how you treat yourself. Not only is this the most efficient way to change your habits long term, but, far more importantly, you deserve nothing less.

> *Embarking on this process doesn't just mark a commitment to planning well, making practical changes and achieving goals, it marks a lifelong commitment to being more kind, compassionate and understanding in how you treat yourself.*

Reminder It may be worth adding some more words (like 'forgiving' and 'committed') to your 'Ways I'm Proud to Be' map, having completed this chapter, if you haven't already.

'What's the Harm?' Map: Example

Example of directly comparing ratings of importance out of ten between the 'What's the Harm?' and 'Why Haven't I Changed Already?' maps.

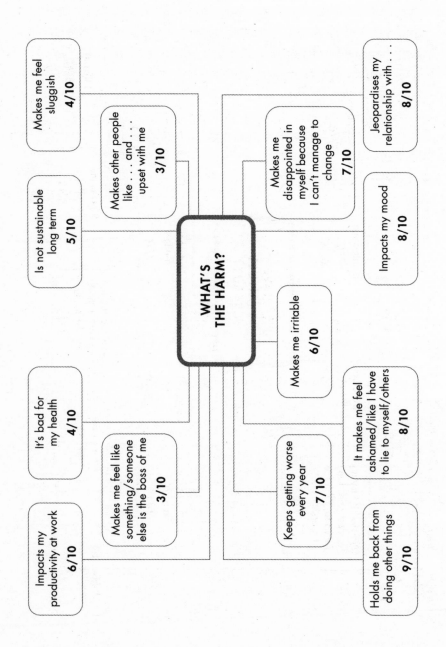

'Why Haven't I Changed Already?' Map: Example

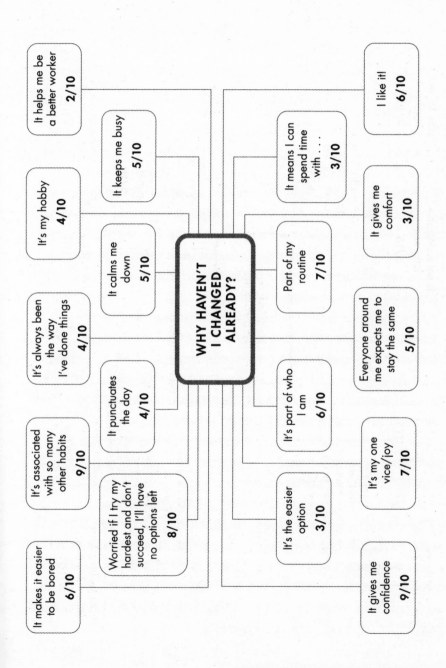

It helps me be a better worker **2/10**

I like it! **6/10**

It keeps me busy **5/10**

It's my hobby **4/10**

It means I can spend time with . . . **3/10**

It gives me comfort **3/10**

It calms me down **5/10**

WHY HAVEN'T I CHANGED ALREADY?

It's always been the way I've done things **4/10**

Part of my routine **7/10**

Everyone around me expects me to stay the same **5/10**

It punctuates the day **4/10**

It's part of who I am **6/10**

It's associated with so many other habits **9/10**

It's my one vice/joy **7/10**

Worried if I try my hardest and don't succeed, I'll have no options left **8/10**

It makes it easier to be bored **6/10**

It's the easier option **3/10**

It gives me confidence **9/10**

CHAPTER 13
WHAT WILL TEST ME?

———

To recap from previous chapters, we are always engaging in habits. So when we change or remove one, we will need to consider what we are doing in its place. If we don't plan well enough for those moments when it's hardest to resist engaging in the undesired habit, we can find ourselves either giving in to short-term discomfort or replacing one unwanted habit with another.

Forewarned is forearmed. So, by first thinking about what generally tends to start those unhelpful internal conversations, and then considering this in the context of our specific plans of change, we can pre-empt our high-risk situations, when we are most likely to lapse. This enables us to decrease the likelihood of being affected by the conditions that make us feel less resilient.

I've found time after time that simply understanding why our habits have emerged (without judgement of whether they're good or bad) is enough to make us change how we behave. The next time we go to do something, even if it's unwanted, there's a connection between mind and body. We can think, 'Ah, there's that behaviour again that I'm trying to change. I know where that comes from, it's left over from when it served me, and now my mind and body are just used to acting that way. I knew this would come, I knew it would test me. I was waiting for this test. I'm ready to deal with it. I'm capable of staying on track with my plan despite it.'

Knowing Your Triggers

We've explored the conversations we have about ourselves that can cause lapse and relapse. Now we will also look at how we anticipate and respond to the high-risk situation itself that can contribute to lapse and relapse. Usually when we unpack things we realise our 'triggers' are a mixture of both our internal conversations and our responses to situations. In this context, a trigger is anything that sparks the desire to engage in habits you're trying to change.

Once I started understanding how and why my habits had emerged, I began to be able to pre-empt my triggers. I would set myself up to be prepared for the day ahead by starting the morning writing out what I expected my mind and body to do that day, based on what they had always done in the past.

'I bet that, even if I manage to stick to my plan, around 6:30pm today I'll start telling myself that I should order a takeaway and binge. If it's raining, or the person I have a meeting with this afternoon annoys me as usual, that may be actually be more like 5:30pm. Initially I'll tell myself that it'll only be one blip off my healthy eating plan, and that I'm capable of getting straight back on track afterwards. But afterwards I'll tell myself that now I've "ruined it" and been "bad" I should have a burger too – and cookies, and crisps. As if it's the last meal I'll ever have. Then I'll probably sit around and feel uncomfortably full, telling myself I'm weak and lazy. Maybe I'll fall asleep on the couch without brushing my teeth.

'The next morning I'll wake up feeling groggy and bloated, which will make me less inclined to shower and make an effort with my appearance, because I'll tell myself I'm not worthy and there's no point in turd-polishing. I'll then drag my feet through the day, getting annoyed at everyone (not least happy-looking people) and starve myself until lunch as a punishment. Then, having caught a glimpse of myself in a toilet mirror between waking and lunch, I'll decide that since I feel so awful already, and I'm so tired, I simply haven't got the energy to deprive myself of a massive lunch. Plus, I'll still be in "being bad" mode. I'll convince myself that soon I'll be back on track and all the delicious

foods in the world will be forbidden. I'll be back in a prison of my own making. So I'll try to convince myself that it's best to eat everything that is delicious.'

Eventually I turned this morning ritual of free-writing my common patterns into a quick twice-daily exercise designed to help me feel less at the mercy of common day-to-day triggers. Many of my clients who had never imagined wanting to or being able to commit to a daily journal-writing practice (let alone a twice-daily one) have really surprised themselves with how long they've kept this up.

'Headline Journal' Exercise Guidance

Adapted from my original free-writing exercise, this is an optional daily practice you can choose to adopt in a bid to speed up the 'increasing self-awareness' element of *The Kindness Method*. I appreciate that it's not for everyone but it can take as little as five minutes and have a quickly noticeable positive impact on your day-to-day life. Although this exercise is still useful when used occasionally, it's undoubtedly most effective when it becomes part of your daily routine.

AM Headline Journal

Every morning, you use the template opposite to make a note of the things you suspect will test you that day. You consider beforehand how you'd like to behave if and when those things do present themselves. Naturally you won't be able to guess everything, but very often we do know the day-to-day things that trigger us and if we gave them more pre-emptive consideration, we could probably anticipate a lot of them beforehand. Then when we're met with them, we feel more in control because we expected them. This may not change how it *feels* to be met with them, but it can absolutely change how we decide to act. Many of my clients have reported that their morning headline journal helped them to avoid acting in ways they'd typically later regret, due to feeling caught off guard.

PM Headline Journal

The evening journal just captures the stuff you didn't guess that morning. It gives you an opportunity to reflect on how you responded to challenging situations and either acknowledge your accomplishment or acknowledge a desire to try a different response next time.

I recommend copying out the template below a few times. Feel free to make the wording more concise or to adapt it (either now or down the line) so it makes most sense to you and your life.

> Date
>
> **AM**
>
> Tasks, Interactions, Thoughts, Feelings, Circumstances or Events
> that may well test me today . . .
> How would I usually respond? . . .
> How could I respond that would make me feel pleasantly surprised with
> myself when I look back on it tonight? . . .
>
> **PM**
>
> Tasks, Interactions, Thoughts, Feelings, Circumstances or Events that have
> tested me today . . .
> What happened? . . .
> How did I respond? . . .
> Do I want to handle it differently if and when it happens again? . . .
> If so, how? . . .

Common Triggers

Some triggers are very obvious – for example, if you're trying not to smoke and people are smoking around you, or offering you cigarettes. Others are more about associations, like smoking after dinner, or with a drink, or during lunch breaks. With the more obvious ones that are in our control, in the short term at least, it's wise to think about how we can avoid them altogether. Using the example of smoking, you may decide not to be around people who you know will be smoking (or drinking) for the first few weeks of giving up, while you get some time under your belt to let your new habits take shape and become normal for you.

Other triggers are more subtle and completely manageable in isolation, but can build up into a high-risk combination of physical and emotional states. Here are a few examples of general triggers. Again, these are examples to get you thinking about your own life and experiences. The more you can recognise your personal ones, the better.

Fatigue

It seems obvious, but we often underestimate the impact that lack of rest or sleep deprivation can have on our mental health and emotional resilience. It is important to ensure, especially in the initial stages of change, that you are sleeping enough. Feeling lethargic can put you on a back foot that starts a stream of internal conversations and behaviours that make it more difficult for you to tolerate emotional and physical discomfort.

Hunger

This is particularly important if you want to change habits around food. So many of the best intentions have been derailed by, for example, going food shopping while hungry. If food is not an issue for you, then simply make sure you are not hungry or thirsty throughout the day. If food is an issue, it's important to remember that while food can be a comfort, the foods and eating styles that you have established as being problematic for you should not be used as excuses to relieve yourself. It's important to 'redefine' your definition of being kind to yourself. Kindness is not succumbing to immediate, short-lived fixes that become less and less effective over time. It's looking at the bigger picture and believing in your ability to push through temporary discomfort in the pursuit of living a more enjoyable life overall. Your aim here is to create the most fertile ground possible on which you can make sound decisions based on achieving your long-term goals and not succumbing to short-term relief.

Stress

Feelings of stress are often something that we want to push away or distract ourselves from as quickly as possible. Often the situations that create stress cannot be avoided. Situations such as financial concerns, professional deadlines and relationship pressures, for example, will not go away simply because we have decided they are not useful to our plans. We can, however, remember that there will never be a 'perfect' time to make ourselves go through a period of change and therefore we will have to face inevitable discomfort. I have noticed that the causes of the kind of stress that lowers resolve differ hugely from person to person. It is important to consider what areas of your life present the most stressful situations for you and to focus your attention on coping strategies to first distract from, then sit with and then eventually manage and relieve that stress long term.

Worry

Rumination and catastrophising often leave us feeling emotionally exhausted and less able to deal with discomfort head-on. Of course, when it comes to anxiety, different people experience it to very different degrees under completely different circumstances. 'Worrying about worrying' is something I struggle with myself.

'Worry Snapshot' Exercise: Collecting Data

Some of my clients now manage elements of anxiety very effectively by keeping a log of how often their worries transpire to be unfounded and use that list to challenge new worries as and when they creep up.

This technique started as a practice I made up for myself to help me maintain perspective and challenge my own assumptions. I would make a note on my phone every time I felt overwhelmed with anxious thoughts. I'd note down what I thought was going on in that moment, and try to capture what I believed to be going on at that time. Then I would look at it later when I felt more calm, and update the entry with what had happened since, noting down times when my assumptions were untrue.

I did this because I had started to notice how often I would look back on days spent worrying and think 'what a waste of time' and 'I can't believe the conclusions I jumped to' and 'I can't believe how worked up I got myself' and 'I can't believe I created such an elaborate story out of nothing' and 'of course it transpired that there was nothing to worry about, as per usual.'

Referring to this ever-growing log of 'Worry Snapshots' helped to provide a reminder of how many times history has proven that my fears were unfounded. I have noticed both in my clients and myself that we often remember the times we worried about something negative happening and it did, yet we seem to forget the many times we worried about something else happening and it didn't!

'Worry Snapshot' Exercise Guidance

If you feel it would be helpful to develop your own log of 'Worry Snapshots', I recommend writing out the headings below in your notebook or on a notes app on your phone.

Part 1

At the time when you feel like you can't stop worrying about something, just quickly note down:

- **What I'm worried about in this moment**
- **What I think is going on**

Then put this away for now.

Part 2

Later on (hours, days or weeks later) when you feel less overwhelmed, go back and for the same entry, ask yourself:

- **Did it transpire that I was making assumptions about the situation that made me worry needlessly?**

Complacency

Success can itself be a trigger. Often clients will come into our sessions really excited to tell me about their successes. Usually this is because we have spent a lot of time discussing, planning, playing out different scenarios and mapping around how they will approach a particularly high-risk, specific situation. The client may come into the room and have barely sat down before they tell me:

'The wedding went so, so well! Even though there was drinking all day and triggers to be unkind to myself were everywhere, I stuck to my plan! At times I was still really tempted to go off track and all the excuses came flooding in, but I looked at my photos of my maps that I have on my phone whenever I went to the loo and I remembered how I would feel the next day if I managed to do what I said. I'm feeling so proud of myself and I can see I've really made changes. All my friends and family

noticed a real change in me too, and said our sessions must be working. It's worked!'

My response usually goes something like this:

'Congratulations, that's wonderful, a well-deserved success. Make sure to add it to your 'What I'm Proud of' map, and any new, high-risk, wedding-specific triggers we hadn't considered should go on your triggers maps too. If I'd told you a few months ago that you'd do what you've done I don't think you'd have believed it, so absolutely acknowledge your hard work.

'Now I really don't want to rain on your parade but it's important to be aware that complacency may creep in now. You are attempting to change years of ingrained habits. This is still far from being your new norm. Don't get me wrong, this is exactly how it looks at the beginning of you spending the rest of your life managing to stick to your plans. But it's really important to assume that you will need to plan the next few times as meticulously as you planned this one, before you assume that this isn't a high-risk situation for you any more. There could be a number of variables we didn't consider, both internally and externally.'

❛ You are attempting to change years of ingrained habits. This is still far from being your new norm.

I react this way to decrease the possibility of either an 'I'm fixed' or 'change is a punishment' mentality creeping in, which may lead to these kinds of internal conversations:

'Wow, I'm all better now! I've completely changed. That's it now, I've proven that everything is different, forever. I'm so strong and proud and resilient, nothing can throw me off track. I don't really need to do all those little things to prepare for high-risk situations or make sure I get loads of sleep or fill out maps. This is who I am now.'

Or:

'Hmmm, how could I celebrate managing to do what I thought I couldn't do? Maybe by treating myself by doing just a little of the things I've managed not to do. Maybe just a bit. Maybe just for a little while . . .'

When complacency leads to lapse, we can become extremely demoralised to realise how easy it is to go back to old, unwanted ways. It is important to remember that your 'old way' hasn't disappeared, it's just stayed where it was when you decided to leave it behind. Over time the new path will be the one you always choose, but the old path is there, and although it moves further and further into the distance as you get more 'changed' time under your belt, is ready for you to step back onto it if you choose to. It's unrealistic to think we can go back to the old path, where everything looks and feels as it did for so many years, and expect ourselves to behave completely differently on it.

'What Will Test Me?' Map Guidance

Now, write 'What Will Test Me?' in the middle of a blank page with a bubble drawn around it. See the example map at the end of the chapter. Then note down what it is that generally causes you to feel stress, worry, become overly tired or have less-than-kind conversations with yourself. Draw a bubble around each entry as you go. What will test your ability to stay on track? Some of these cues may help:

Thinking . . .	Doing . . .	Seeing . . .
Feeling . . .	Discovering . . .	Realising . . .
Being exposed to . . .	Smelling . . .	Touching . . .
Remembering . . .	Saying . . .	Hearing . . .
Meeting . . .		

Once you have completed your 'What Will Test Me?' map, read back over it and consider what you currently do to relieve, avoid, change or address these possible scenarios. Are any of those methods both effective and ones you want to carry on employing? If yes, could you do more of them as part of your ultimate change plan? As with the exercises before, if these questions bring about any realisations, make a note of them for your own reference.

'What Will Test Me?' Map: Example

This map is a sample for guidance purposes only.
Make yours personal to you, in your own handwriting.

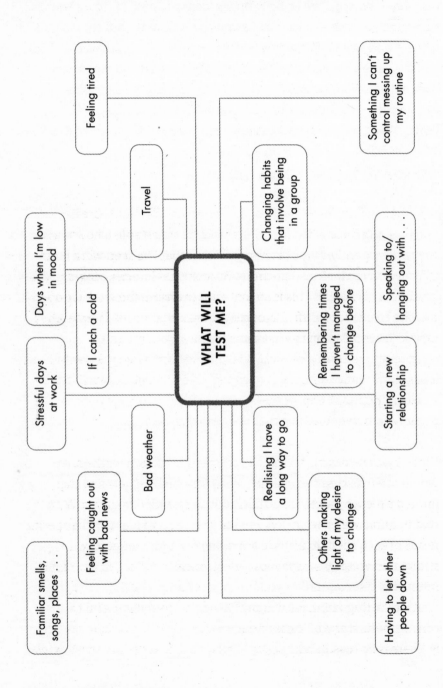

CHAPTER 14
FUTURE MATTERS
___

In addiction treatment, practitioners often use different assessment and profiling tools with their clients in order to establish how ready they are, currently, to make changes. Some that I've seen work most effectively draw on concepts from Motivational Interviewing, such as 'readiness to change'. This is so that we can ensure the work we do to prepare clients for a difficult journey ahead is tailor-made for each individual. In addition to looking at practical support and considerations, from a motivational perspective, when we want to assess how ready someone is to change, we can look at two things:

1 How important it is for them to change?
2 How confident are they that they can change?

When I was delivering training to frontline addiction workers, we would often discuss the realities of our strained budgets and the limited time we had to work therapeutically with our clients. With that in mind, we were always keen to find ways to identify the specific needs of each client as quickly as possible, in order to prepare and get straight down to using the most effective evidence-based tools and interventions required.

As a starting point, with many clients I've found it useful to consider which one of these variations best describes where the client is. There is no reason why we can't adapt approaches like these, which are most commonly used by practitioners assessing 'readiness to change', for ourselves, to give us insight into which areas to focus on developing when we want to make changes.

High Importance and Low Confidence

This is the profile used to describe someone who urgently needs to make changes. Common reasons for change being very important have, in my experience, included deteriorating health or medical diagnoses, social services involvement, engagement with criminal justice services, the impending arrival of a child or another imminent big life change. As such, it's likely to be a waste of time at best, and patronising at worst, to keep hammering home what the consequences are if they don't make changes. They are fully aware.

However, the 'low confidence' element may mean that they have little (if any) faith that they will be able to change. Again, to generalise, I have seen this be because of guilt and shame around clients' behaviour to date, extremely low self-esteem and negative self-talk, and in many cases as a consequence of experiences of abuse and neglect. When they come into contact with a practitioner for the first time, it is not uncommon for some clients to be unable to say anything they like about themselves or recall an occasion when they felt capable or that they'd achieved something.

In my practice I would always bring the client's attention to the fact that they had found the courage to turn up and ask for help, and therefore had demonstrated a range of strengths. Secondly, a large proportion of a strengths map can be filled out by breaking down the skills required to sustain a life in addiction. As my mentor Ray Jenkins (knower of all things recovery) always reminded me, it's hard to sustain a life in recovery but it's harder to sustain a life in addiction. A lot of clients would wake up every morning and find a way to acquire their drug of choice, with or without money. They would find ways to travel across London, negotiate prices and put various plans in place to ensure that they didn't withdraw. Not only was drawing on these skills useful when we would discuss potential employment, for example, but also it reminded them of their resilience. In addition, very often these clients had no fixed abode. Through the winter they would have to arrange a bed in a hostel if they weren't sleeping outside, and all the while they were often dealing with being stigmatised, and may sometimes have been victims of physical and sexual violence, too.

You can see that this is not the description of someone who cannot withstand discomfort or someone who has not demonstrated strengths and achievements. It's someone who needs support in realizing that these same qualities are transferable into a life lived in a culture of recovery.

Low Importance and High Confidence

This was a client profile I saw a lot when I was working with regular cannabis users. For a while, I delivered a weekly support group for young people who, for various reasons, had been coerced into attending by parents or schools. Some of them were able to do what was required to pass exams and fulfil other people's day-to-day expectations of them. A lot of the time, however, parents and teachers had noticed their motivation levels gradually dropping, plus they naturally weren't happy that the young people were buying and using an illegal drug.

Very often members of the group would tell me that they could stop smoking whenever they wanted to. They were adamant that they were not addicted to cannabis and that it wasn't currently impacting their lives in a way that was problematic. In many ways, they were right. But it wasn't the current state of affairs that myself and other adults were most concerned about, as much as what would happen the next year or the year after, when more was required of them academically and professionally, and their tolerance to the drug had invariably increased, almost certainly leading them to smoke more.

In the case of a lot of these young people, I saw that they were able to complete maps designed to capture their achievements without too much trouble. They were used to being regularly assessed in various ways at school and given a number of opportunities to develop and nurture their skills and strengths. They were reminded of their achievements and regularly encouraged by teachers. Plus, some of them weren't daily users and even sometimes went weeks without using cannabis, so they were very aware that they weren't dealing with serious physical dependency.

So, as a practitioner, my time wasn't best spent employing tools and approaches to help them believe they could stop smoking, but rather to draw to their attention why it might be important to do so. If not now, then eventually. In order to do that, we would discuss how much their tolerance had increased since they first started smoking and hypothesise about what that meant for the next couple of years – at the very least financially. We would talk about whether they wanted to be drug users into adulthood, and if the answer was no (as it most often was), then at what point they saw themselves changing. In this way, rather than focus on what was bad about what they were doing now, we discussed what kind of life they'd be excited to have in five years' time and the focus, qualifications or finances they would need to get there. In this way, they often moved their motivation from 'low importance' to 'high importance'.

High Importance and High Confidence

This person is best positioned to start making changes from a 'readiness to change' perspective. This is where we ideally want clients to be when they embark on their process. I often saw clients who fit this profile upon release from prison, where they had engaged well with group programmes, had a long period of abstinence, were feeling the benefits from every angle and very much wanted to stay on track.

Low Importance and Low Confidence

The person who fits this profile might be someone who doesn't see many urgent reasons to change and even if they did, doesn't believe they could do it. Arguably, this person is the most challenging to work with from a practitioner's point of view, but even so, it is far from impossible to support them in making big changes.

Back to You: Increasing Importance to Match Confidence

Having looked at how self-sabotage tends to work and the importance of having kinder conversations with yourself, you have already adopted ways to address the 'confidence' element of these categories. Now you need to make sure that you feel the 'importance' is as high as possible. With that in mind, in the next section of this process we will look at:

1 Bringing about urgency to change
2 Making sure you're making changes for reasons that are meaningful to you

Before we move on to the next couple of chapters and complete maps that are designed to bring about a sense of urgency and to challenge any delayed action, I'd like you to start getting excited about the future you want and identify what elements of change both specific to and surrounding your habit are most important to you.

'How It's Most Important for Me to Be' Exercise Guidance

For this exercise, choose at least one of these questions to answer in as much detail as you can. Take time to really paint a clear picture in your response. Copy the question or questions into your notebook and then write down your answers.

- If a stranger (who could somehow hear your thoughts) followed you around for one whole day in twelve months' time, how would you like them to describe your thoughts and behaviours in a way that's different to how they are now?

- In terms of your obvious habits and how you feel and treat yourself, engage with the world and your general outlook on life, what would you like your loved ones to observe has changed in you, six months on from starting to apply *The Kindness Method*?

- Imagine you and everyone you love and respect are sitting in a cinema. You are all watching a film in which the lead actor plays you and depicts your day-to-day life one year from now. They act out how you deal with challenging people and situations. They're dressed how you dress, stand how you stand, and make the same choices you make. Write a description of the character in that film.

- Imagine your much younger self was looking through a window into your work or home life six or twelve months from now. They've come to see what they will be like as an adult, in a sort of *A Christmas Carol* scene. What would you like them to see you doing? What kind of scene would reassure them and make them feel proud that, when it comes to the habits you have control over, things have turned out great?

CHAPTER 15
WHAT'S THE DIFFERENCE?

This chapter includes two maps which you will set out in a similar structure. However, the content will be very different. The idea is to project into the future and bring about a sense of urgency by considering what life might look like if you don't change, directly compared to what it would look like if you do.

'Life if I Don't Make Changes' Map Guidance

For this map I'd like you to first write 'Life if I Don't Make Changes' in the centre of a blank page. Then, I'd like you to write a future date under this title and draw a bubble around both together.

For most clients who want to make a general range of changes across various areas of their lives, I recommend choosing a future date six or twelve months from either today's date or from the date you wrote your 'Snapshot Letter'.

Don't worry, it won't take six or twelve months for things to get easier and for you to make big changes. You will be celebrating milestones within this time and enjoying the rewards of progress and achieving your short-term goals. This exercise is specifically designed to help you project further into the future and challenge the 'I'll start on Monday' thinking. Whether you choose six or twelve months is up to you – it depends on the changes you want to make and how quickly you feel it's realistic for you to make them. Sometimes clients want to stop smoking ahead of the birth of a child, procrastinate less ahead of a set of work deadlines, or even train for a marathon. In these cases they have an even more specific date to put in the middle of their map. See the example map at the end of the chapter.

Now, start to populate this map with words and sentences describing how you think things will look across your life if you don't manage to make the changes you'd like to make. Draw a bubble around each new entry as you go. Consider these three questions to focus you:

1 How will you feel?
2 What relevant events may have taken place by then?
3 What kind of things will you be saying to yourself?

When you're finished, put this map to one side for a moment.

'Life if I Do Make Changes' Map Guidance

Now, I'd like you to recreate the structure of the previous map again, writing down the same future date you chose before. The only difference is that you write 'Life if I Do Make Changes' in the centre of the map. Again, see the example map at the end of the chapter.

Do bear in mind what you know now about motivation and the interplay between habits. For example, stopping smoking may not be a professional goal so much as a health or social one, but having managed not to smoke for a year is likely to make you feel more capable, which in turn may well mean you feel more confident to do things, including professionally, that you once doubted you could.

When completing the second map, be careful not to simply write the alternative also phrased as a negative, but write it as a new positive. For example, if in the first map you've written, 'I'll be telling myself I'm weak,' don't write, 'I won't be telling myself I'm weak,' in the second. Instead write, 'I'll be telling myself how strong and capable I am.' Bringing some urgency into your plans in this way can prove effective in a scaremongering sort of 'look how bad things will get if you don't change' kind of way. But, as we now know, shock tactics and concentrating on negatives can get people going but they don't sustain change in the long term. For that, we need to imagine a life that sounds more enjoyable, not just less negative.

Getting Excited About the Future

The 'Life if I Do Make Changes' map should have helped you get pretty excited about how things could be looking and feeling for you in the not-so-distant future, and how many areas of your life could be improved. It's also a useful tool for envisaging the kind of life you want in general, and asking yourself questions around your valued life direction.

> The Kindness Method *isn't only about isolating and changing specific habits. It is about working towards creating a life on purpose (and of purpose) that excites you.*

Addiction treatment taught me that when practical, sustained changes seemed to be made rapidly by a client after a number of unsuccessful attempts, on closer inspection it tended to be a culmination of various different approaches, tools and interventions that all eventually clicked into place and started to work in harmony. Regardless of the individual or the drug involved, the materials from which these tools were fashioned were compassion, forgiveness and kindness towards oneself.

Affirmations – Bringing the Future into the Present

One exercise that some clients have found extremely useful is to write down a list of affirmations which combine qualities they already have and things they already are with things they aspire to have and to be. While trying to lose weight, I created a list of affirmations that I would repeat every morning to myself out loud in the mirror. At first it felt really silly but after a while, real shifts started taking place in how I would engage with the world around me in general. After a while, I really started to behave like someone who had already achieved the things I aspired to. 'Fake it till you make it' is a term I hear often. I personally have found that before we aspire to that, we could take a moment to acknowledge that in many ways there's little faking required because in many ways we often have 'made it.'

One of my clients wanted to address her co-dependent thoughts and assumptions that manifested themselves in people-pleasing, comparing herself to others, and placing a lot of focus on what other people thought of her. She told me that she felt all these were getting out of control, and she realised she would go overboard giving her time and attention to others and neglect herself in the process. She found that this was not only detrimental to building a positive relationship with herself and maintaining balanced relationships with friends and family, it was also holding her back from creating healthy romantic relationships. We identified together that this came from a place of fear that she wasn't 'good enough' and that perhaps she would be rejected if she wasn't always serving a purpose of some kind. These assumptions and associated behaviours had developed in her early childhood. She told me she was tired of living her life through the eyes of others as a result of these assumptions and that she had lost the sense of who she was when others weren't feeding back that she was an 'okay' person. She also felt that her compulsive, excessive use of social media and her phone wasn't helping the situation.

Her previous attempts to change things had included suddenly drawing up harsh and rash boundaries with loved ones, isolating herself from friends and completely deleting all social media (extreme measures that she couldn't keep up and which didn't actually address the issues around her not feeling good about herself).

What she found was that each time she hastily tried to 'fix' herself this way, she would then worry what people thought about her new behaviour. She would ruminate over whether people had noticed her withdraw and the fact that she'd stopped posting on social media. She wondered if they now thought that she considered herself 'better' than them. In other words, the underlying issue of her co-dependent behaviour wasn't being addressed. Her low self-esteem and inability to envisage a life that was different still saw her assessing her value through the eyes of others. She would beat herself up what she called the 'double-tick tumbleweed of terror' every time she posted on a WhatsApp group and no one responded. She would tell herself stories about what must have happened, that she'd offended people or that they'd all turned against her.

For this client, affirmations read out loud in the morning made all the difference. She said that hearing very fair, very logical statements read out loud, with purpose, helped her when she was faced with a 'triggering' scenario. After seeing her make such amazing changes, I now tell my clients that their Affirmations Lists can be a mixture of:

- An emotional wish-list
- A to-do list
- Things they already have and are

Here is a collection of affirmations from the client in this example, for inspiration:

I love myself unconditionally

I am worthy of being loved unconditionally

I take my time to react to internal and external triggers, and I let the dust settle before I make decisions about what works for me

I remember people have their own problems and I don't take things personally when they don't act the way I want them to

I don't always need to appear to be 'right' in the eyes of others

I make healthy choices for myself every day

I respect myself and trust my instincts and decisions before those of others. I know what's right for me

I'm able to ask others to meet my needs or desires

I look only to myself to provide a sense of safety

I set healthy boundaries that feel authentic, realistic and sustainable to me

I am not better or worse than anyone else

I believe that all those around me are capable of taking care of themselves

I only offer advice when I'm asked for it

I protect my life choices and only share what I choose to

I don't use gifts and favours to make people like me or give me attention

I don't have to be needed in order to have a relationship with others

I don't demand that my needs be met by others

I don't pretend to agree with others to make them approve of me

I believe that I deserve true intimacy in a relationship

I accept all my feelings as a part of who I am

I know when to slow down and take one thing at a time

I have so much to be grateful for

I am a caring and conscientious friend and family member

I enjoy and appreciate the people in my life

I allow myself to enjoy the happiness that I truly deserve

I have achieved far more than I could ever have imagined as a child

I genuinely believe that the only behaviour I have any control over is my own

I trust my emotions and thoughts, and I make good decisions

I can identify and express my feelings honestly

I grow more and more confident every day

I intuitively know how to handle situations which used to baffle me

I am resilient and capable

I am patient. I trust that the right people and opportunities will come to me

I am sharp, witty, energetic, bright and ambitious

I am calm, composed and wise

I am autonomous and independent in my opinions and behaviours

I am beautiful

I often leave a great impression on people

I know what I need from others and what I can give myself

I have a beautiful home which makes me feel safe and represents who I am

I am conscious of what I enjoy and why it feels right for me

Challenging situations excite me and help me grow
I love my life and whatever today may bring, I always remember
I am enormously lucky
I see the lessons in my experiences and I'm grateful for them
I deserve to be treated well
My positive outlook attracts positive opportunities
I am competent, intelligent and able
I believe in myself
I surround myself with people who bring out the best in me
I am always growing and developing
What matters most is not what happens, but how I react and what
I believe about it.

Tip if you think it would be useful to create your own list of affirmations, it can help to reflect on your 'Ways I'm Happy to Be' map, 'Things I'm Proud of' map and 'Life If I Do Make Changes' map.

'Life if I Don't Make Changes' Map: Example

This map is a sample for guidance purposes only.
Make yours personal to you, in your own handwriting.

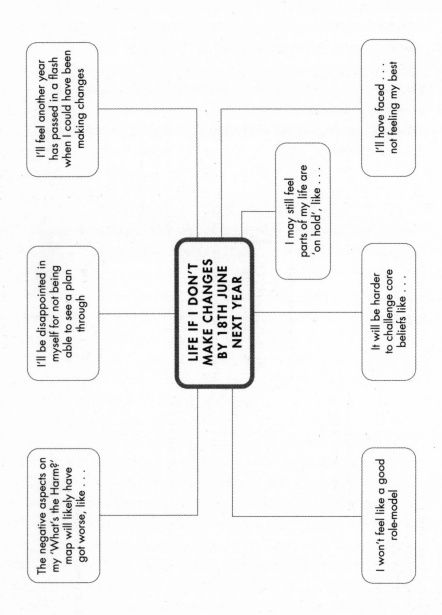

'Life if I Do Make Changes' Map: Example

This map is a sample for guidance purposes only.

Make yours personal to you, in your own handwriting.

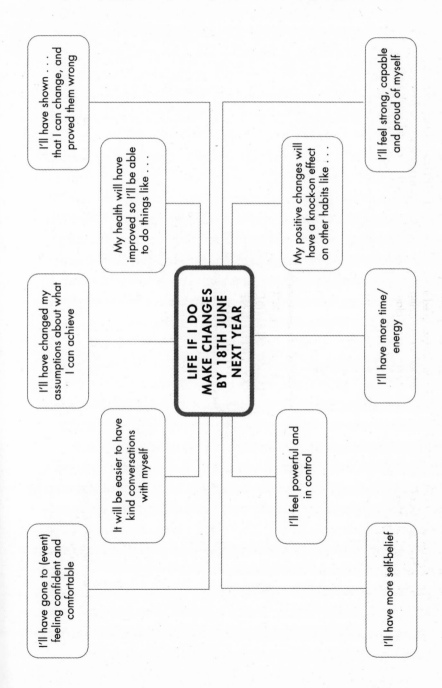

CHAPTER 16
THE PLAN

——

The time has finally come to start formulating your plan. When you put this plan into action will be up to you. Some plans will need a bit more advance thought than others to make sure they have the best likelihood of being sustainable. First I will provide some tips and address common stumbling blocks and challenges before helping you to create a plan of your own at the end of the chapter.

Set a Review Date

Before you do anything else, set a review date. Everyone's plans are different so you can choose your own date, but I suggest you begin with reviewing your plan every three weeks or so, and tweak if necessary. You will find that as you work out what does and doesn't work for you, the gaps between tweaks will increase until, eventually, new habits begin to come much more naturally and become your new norm.

If prior to your review date you decide your plan is 'too easy', it can be a good idea to carry on as planned regardless. You need to test it out under a range of circumstances, so just let life happen around your changes and see how it goes. Then if by your first review date it's still too easy and your resolve hasn't been tested at all, you can then make it more challenging.

If getting to this stage has made you want to put off the 'action' part of this process, please observe your inclination to avoid the discomfort of imagining discomfort. Before I used this process, knowing that it was 'go-time' would be enough to make me want to indulge in a last blow-out binge. Working in drug addiction, I learned that often this was what my clients would do the night prior to checking into residential rehab! Remember, you're not making changes because you've been 'bad'. You can go back to doing whatever you like for as long as you like. But if you've got this far, I'm thinking by now you probably want to change and see results as soon as possible.

Formulating a Realistic Plan

A good rule of thumb for your initial plan is for it to be enough of a change to challenge you, but not so much of a change that you doubt whether you can manage it. The most important part of this very first plan is not to make huge changes – it's simply to do what you said you were going to do. If you achieve this, then when you come to create a more challenging plan three weeks later your mindset then will be very different, and the likelihood of you sticking to a more ambitious plan long term will have increased. Your 'Things I'm Proud of' map will also be filling up as a result.

These initial short-term goals aren't there to facilitate profound changes. They're there to challenge the status quo enough for you to:
- Start practising 'turning up the volume' on your thinking patterns, interpretation of situations, self-sabotage and excuse-making
- Start appreciating how strongly your habits have a hold on you and dictate your day-to-day choices
- Give yourself an opportunity to increase your confidence in yourself and your capabilities so you feel worthy and ambitious when setting your next set of goals
- Give yourself an initial structure from which to observe your inclinations and provide a benchmark for following your plans

- Remind yourself of the joy, energy and resilience that come with proving yourself (and others, if this is important to you) wrong about what you're capable of

During stage one (explained opposite), minimise your chances of being exposed to triggers wherever possible with distraction and delay techniques and put short-term activities and strategies in place for times of boredom and other high-risk situations. Although reacting to uncomfortable situations by avoiding them is not an attitude you want to continue subscribing to for a lifetime, in this stage it can work to your advantage.

The Different Stages of the Process

The planning process is personal and unique. It will differ massively from person to person, not just depending on specific goals but also in terms of timings and how to measure outcomes. It will also differ depending on each individual's level of confidence at the beginning of the process. So I won't tell you what deadlines or review dates to choose, or what particular behaviours you need to demonstrate to show that you've entered a new stage. I will, however, tell you how you should generally be feeling about how the plan is going.

Stage One

Wow, I've managed to keep it up! I've really surprised myself and I'm feeling strong and proud. That wasn't as difficult as I thought it would be. Changing for good is definitely a realistic possibility. I think I can gradually make things a bit more challenging without worrying they'll throw me off track. I'm starting to notice when I'm not speaking kindly to myself. I'm noticing my inner dialogue a lot more. I still need to plan a lot, though, and make sure I don't get stressed or book in anything that might make the process any harder. Even though most days have been manageable, there have been quite a few close calls and I still have to keep things 'doable'. I expect short-term discomfort and I'm taking it one minute at a time, pushing through, safe in the knowledge it will only be like this at the beginning.

Stage Two

This is the plan that works for me. I'm not just feeling more confident and capable but I'm also finding it less of a novelty to be behaving this way. This doesn't need any more tweaking. Carrying on as I am now will get me to where I want to be. The plan's been tested under various different circumstances (some I expected, some I didn't) and the close calls are getting fewer and fewer. I deal with my triggers by engaging in sustainable habits that I consider kind and healthy. When cravings, impulses or unhelpful internal negotiations come about, I find myself increasingly able to observe them and be still, instead of making excuses or needing external coping strategies to distract from them. When I'm presented with a high-risk situation I didn't expect, I am able to deal with it by referring to my maps, refreshing my memory and because I am generally more resilient and feeling the benefits of my changes. If I have a craving or impulse to succumb to short-term relief from emotional discomfort or boredom, I don't urgently have to find something else to do or seek external support. I am able to do nothing but observe it and challenge myself to sit through it. I'm also noticing life improvements I hadn't considered when I made the plan.

Stage Three

The changes I wanted to make are now my norm and it's extremely rare for me to feel tempted to go back to old ways. Even if I do, these temptations are just internal debates that don't turn into behaviours. Until I want to create a plan for another habit one day, I will maintain my current habits and each day become more aware of even my very subtle triggers. I commit to many tiny daily practices that promote self-care, bring about kinder conversations with myself and generally build my self-esteem. I'm aware of my own very specific triggers and with each year, regardless of what specific habit I want to change, I build more insight into what works for me. Regardless of how normal my new habits seem, every now and then I look at the maps I made at the beginning and reflect on how far I've come. I know I need to do this to keep my self-esteem high and keep any long-term complacency traps at bay.

Managing the Initial Stages

The idea of initially having shorter plans with more frequent reviews is influenced by a concept called 'sobriety sampling', which is an intervention used in some approaches to addiction treatment*. It involves a client giving themselves an opportunity to experience complete sobriety by abstaining for a limited, agreed-upon amount of time. This way they have time to realise some unexpected positive impacts of their sobriety. Similar thinking applies to the effectiveness of 'don't drink/smoke for one month' initiatives.

By focusing on the short-term, we're less likely to overwhelm ourselves with triggering potentially self-sabotaging thoughts like,

---

* Sobriety sampling is a technique from the Community Reinforcement Approach (Myers and Miller, 2001) that is used to encourage clients to consider trying a period of abstinence. The research evidence suggests that those who achieve a period of sobriety are more likely to benefit from treatment (Project Match Research Group, 1997).

'Is this how I'll have to be for the rest of my life?!' I heard someone say once that, 'In order to drive a hundred miles in the dark, you only need to see one metre in front of you at a time. All the while you're getting closer and closer to your ultimate destination.'

One of my clients wanted to cut down his alcohol intake. He decided that his initial three-week plan would involve choosing two nights per week when he could drink a specified amount of white wine. His plan also included details like 'not drinking Sunday nights' and 'no drinking two nights in a row'. He had established that when he drank on Sunday evenings, he felt sluggish and less resilient on Mondays, the very day he needed the most energy because, well, it's Monday. He decided that each Sunday he would decide which two days he'd like to pick that week, depending on social plans and what he had on the next day.

Of course, there were occasions when this client would have already 'used up' his two nights by the time Saturday night came around and something would come up that he really wanted to go to. I'm afraid that under these circumstances, the process required him to miss out. Most likely there will be times when we feel we are depriving ourselves, especially in the early stages when we have to be unbudging about our plans. In these situations, I often say to clients, 'If the way you think you will feel and will speak to yourself after having lapsed is likely to be worse than the way you'll feel if you miss out on the night out, then that's your answer.' There are always going to be crosses to bear and sacrifices to make. This is simply a part of changing ingrained habits.

It will be difficult at times not to trivialise the process or keep putting things off until the next Monday, or after Christmas, or after a wedding or holiday. There will always be something. On these occasions I ask the client to look at their 'Life if I Do Make Changes' map and remember that the date they've chosen is coming around just as quickly whether they make changes or not.

In this case, my client didn't go out on Saturdays if he had used up his 'drinking nights', but he did start waiting until later in the week to assign them, just in case something came up. He also knew he would be playing in a cricket match on Sunday two weeks from the date of starting the plan. He identified this as a high-risk situation for various reasons, including the drinking culture associated with these events.

Get Straight Back in the Saddle

Having pre-empted the likelihood of him having an unhelpful, self-sabotaging conversation with himself about having deviated from his plan, we made sure that he put everything in place for that following Monday after the cricket match to ensure he would be as kind to himself as possible, thereby decreasing the likelihood of the exception he had made throwing him completely off track, just because of a story he told himself about what it meant.

On the previous Friday he made sure that he didn't have a big backlog of work to face on Monday. He bought healthy, delicious food for dinner on Monday night and invited a friend who wasn't a regular drinker round to watch a film he'd been meaning to see for a while. He also expected the bullying, self-sabotaging debates to be louder on Monday, and he was able to welcome them with a knowing 'Yeah, yeah, I knew this was coming, I'm pushing through anyway, carry on if you like' attitude. That night, when he didn't go to the pub, he added it to some of his relevant maps, and by Tuesday it was like he'd never gone off plan. And that is the key to relapse management. In the words of Miles Davis, 'If you hit a wrong note, it's the next note you play that determines if it's good or bad.'

We made a list of the things this client could do in the early stages during his non-drinking evenings (before he started, he was drinking between three and five nights a week, on average). Initially, he really wanted to go to the gym most nights (a lot of people seem to think this is the thing to start doing). That would have been fine if he was physically fit, but he wasn't. So the gym wasn't going to be a fun, easy experience for him. In addition, it could have been counterproductive if he woke up the day after his first visit, aching all over his body. He could have started 'taking it easy on himself' or rewarding himself by drinking on an evening when he'd planned not to. So he made a list of things he could do, at least in the short term, to ease the boredom until he got some time under his belt that he felt protective of. These included:

- Reading
- Visiting museums
- Filling out maps and journals
- Long baths
- Watching documentaries
- Researching guitar lessons
- Cooking
- Listening to podcasts
- Getting early nights
- Planning non-drinking ways to celebrate my achievements
- Going for walks in areas of London I'm not familiar with
- Doing easy, everyday house chores so they don't build up
- Catching up over Skype with friends who've moved away
- Researching my next holiday

The whole concept of change can feel very high risk, filled with its own triggers. Be on the lookout for any excuse – internal or external – to make you want to pick the more familiar road.

Some clients email me in between sessions to let me know they have changed their plans of action. Not because they want me to reply necessarily, but rather to declare and clarify their intentions. Sometimes in the early stages it's because they don't trust themselves not to keep making convenient impromptu tweaks to the plan. It's also harder to justify excuses that don't make much sense when you're explaining them out loud to someone else!

Sometimes, however, our carefully laid plans will change in a way that is out of our control and if that happens when we're not feeling resilient, we can find ourselves suddenly in a high-risk situation.

The reality of needing to change your day-to-day plan for unforeseen reasons can itself be a trigger for the common self-sabotaging conversation: 'Oh, I've ruined this plan now, I'll have to put time aside to create a new one.' Before I started challenging my excuses, a lapse and sustained relapse would often come about because in one moment of hunger or boredom I'd believe an absurd story I told myself: that one tiny, unavoidable digression from my plan meant the kiss of death for my entire process and that all my hard work up to that point now counted for nothing.

A common example of this happened during the first week of one of my plans. Things were going well and I was feeling good about my progress. I'd decided to go to a free yoga class I'd seen advertised. I knew it was important to be occupied that evening, so I commuted in the rain on an empty stomach, after a long day at work, to try something completely new. Even though these external factors had the potential to be triggers, I didn't seem to care much about the hunger and rain. I probably thought: 'Maybe hunger and rain don't even bother me any more. I'm changed. I'm fixed! This plan is really working. I'm going to yoga, for goodness sake! Who knows, maybe I'll become obsessed with it and become a yoga instructor!'

Then, when I arrived, I was told the class had been cancelled because the instructor was ill. All of a sudden, I cared very much indeed about being hungry and tired and drenched. My initial enthusiasm wasn't built on strong enough foundations; my contingency plans weren't formed properly and my thinking patterns weren't based on rational reasoning.

'That's that then. The plan wasn't foolproof enough,' I thought. 'I'll have to go back to the drawing board. In the meantime, I'm drenched and tired and deserve to deal with my hunger with things I won't be able to eat when the new, perfect plan is created tomorrow ...'

Even now, I sometimes catch myself starting to entertain a story like this as if it makes any sense. If it's not practical to write things down and I'm feeling particularly vulnerable, and like I can suspend my disbelief for these fictions, I make myself put forward a compelling and rational argument – out loud. It then sounds like a friend is talking to me, hoping that an intelligent person will reflect back to them whether what they are saying makes sense. And usually that friend, frankly, sounds absurd – to think that a minor, unavoidable deviation from their action plan justifies a sabotage of all their efforts, sending them back on a spiral of lapse and potentially relapse!

Sometimes I actually laugh at myself when I hear out loud what used to make sense in my head. Now when I hear my inner voice come out with things like this I think:

'Of course you still think like that, you've been doing it for years. But that's ridiculous. Just go home and eat something healthy. Watch some TV you like or sit and do absolutely nothing, but do look at all the reasons you've written detailing how important it is that you don't lapse. Someone you don't know cancelling a yoga class is just not enough of a reason to go completely off track. Getting to where you want to be is more important than that. Your plans are laid on stronger foundations.'

I appreciate that sometimes, regardless of how carefully we research and plan, we can't stick to our plans as we'd hoped to, even in the short-term. Life will throw things at us that are unavoidable. When that happens I ask you to consider these two questions:

- Does my inability to achieve this one goal I set myself have anything to do with my ability to achieve all the rest of them?
- If I was tasked with explaining to someone else why circumstances have made it impossible for me to continue with this aspect of my plan for a short period of time, would my argument be convincing?

Working on Your Personal Development Goals

If the main area you want to change concerns a habit that is hard to measure, with no obvious visible improvements – such as addressing low self-esteem or catastrophic thinking (as opposed to habits like stopping smoking, using your phone less, spending less, exercising more and so on), then create your plan around a commitment to daily practices that puts time aside for self-development.

This can include things like:

- Free-writing every morning to set intentions and pre-empt the situations and people that are likely to make you doubt yourself

- Reading daily affirmations aloud (bear in mind things like this will need to include a clear instruction to 'write out affirmations to use' as part of your plan)
- Doing exercises like moving paperclips from one pocket to another each time you catch yourself saying something mean to yourself
- Ten minutes of guided meditation each morning, perhaps using free apps or YouTube videos, of which there are plenty available (note again that these things will involve preparation. For instance, finding videos with voices that you like listening to, so you don't give up on this idea because you 'winged it' and ended up listening to someone whose voice really annoys you)
- Completing maps from *The Kindness Method*
- Committing to spending twenty minutes (or however long you can put aside) to do something you do for no other reason than your enjoyment of it. And commit to keeping this plan with yourself the same way you would commit to keeping a plan you had with someone else

Don't Make Your Changes Too Extreme

Changing habits around smoking, drinking and food are all things where I will sometimes ask clients that they try to use the tactic of putting something additional in place as opposed to immediately taking something away. Most of my clients want to start making practical changes straight away, but without adding to a habit first this can be very challenging. For example, if you're used to spending your breaks at work smoking a cigarette, maybe initially make that half a cigarette and a herbal tea or a glass of water. That way, when you next review your progress you'll find you are well on your way to creating a new association with your breaks. Then your next plan could involve rotating between the two and reducing gradually.

If you're anything like me, your initial impulse will be to abstain altogether. And for some, of course, this can work. But please remember that doing it as gently as possible usually saves time overall.

Always Look at the Bigger Picture

This is something I discussed while delivering training to male prisoners, many of whom had been arrested for dealing illegal drugs. One of the purposes of the day was to encourage them to consider their employment options upon release.

At first, they would often tell me that no legal job was going to provide them with the income that dealing did. When they told me how much they were earning over a three-month period, I was inclined to agree (not least because it was about four times what I was earning). That said, many of them were in a revolving-door cycle, a pattern of being released for a few months and then finding themselves back in prison over and over again. Some films and documentaries had given me the impression that each of these young men was overseeing a sophisticated drug-dealing operation from inside prison, with vast networks of colleagues holding the fort until they were back to collect their profits. On speaking to them it would become clear that this really wasn't the case.

So that meant that during the periods they were in prison, they didn't have an income from drug dealing. I would bring to their attention that yes, perhaps when they isolated a three-month period they were earning a lot. But when we calculated an average of their earnings over a couple of years (counting in the fact that big chunks of time were spent earning nothing), they were often surprised to see how low their annual income was.

It can be similar if we look at something like a plan for stopping smoking. Yes, you may want to stop altogether right now and you may keep it up for two weeks, maybe more. But if you set yourself up to lapse and relapse, then the number of cigarettes you smoke over six months may well be more than the number you'd have smoked if you made the process more easy and gradual. On balance, gentle, considered shifts are the better bet for getting where you want to be and staying there.

So for your first plan, the preparation you've done is psychologically and emotionally very important and integral to creating lasting change. But it's impossible to take into consideration every single high-risk scenario, external factor or how you will feel physically. The best we can do is remember that it's up to us how we react to those things and set ourselves up to have fair, kind conversations with ourselves when they occur. If you keep completing your maps and journals regularly, in a few months you will have more high-risk situations and sensations recorded than you could ever imagine at this stage. Copy the statements opposite out into your notebook and fill in the gaps to personalise your plan.

Formulating Your Plan

I will start my plan on . . . , once I've done all the preparation required, such as . . .

I'm committing to . . . (explain your plan in as much detail as possible) . . . times per week on . . . (insert days, times)

My non-negotiable rules for this plan are . . .

This is what 'being on track' or 'being in active recovery' will look like for me . . .

This is what a 'lapse' will look like for me . . .

Unavoidable exceptions to my plan which are out of my control are . . . (I commit to not adding any more to this list after the day I start my plan)

If/when these exceptions occur, I will ensure they don't cause me to lapse by . . .

In the event that I do lapse (and this is not to be seen as permission to do so), I will make sure I get back on track immediately by . . .

In the event that I do lapse I will not make the situation worse by . . .

The thoughts, feelings, people and situations that are likely to make me want to give up are . . .

The things I will do in moments when I want to give up are . . .

I will celebrate sticking to my plan for three weeks by . . .

The date I review this plan will be . . .

Review

The bits that worked in the last plan were . . .

The bits that didn't work so well were . . .

The things I'm proud of myself for are . . .

The things I now know I need to include in my next plan are . . .

High-risk situations I didn't expect included . . .

My new three-week plan involves committing to . . . (explain your plan in as much possible detail as possible) . . . times per week on . . . (insert days, times)

My non-negotiable rules for this plan are . . .

This is what 'being on track' or 'in recovery', will look like for me ...

This is what a 'lapse' will look like for me ...

Unavoidable exceptions to my plan which are out of my control are ... (I commit to not adding any more to this list after the day I start my plan)

If/when these exceptions occur, I will ensure they don't cause me to lapse by ...

In the event that I do lapse (and this is not to be seen as permission to do so), I will make sure I get back on track immediately by ...

In the event that I do lapse, I will not make the situation worse by ...

The thoughts, feelings, people and situations that are likely to make me want to give up are ...

The things I will do in moments when I want to give up are ...

I will celebrate sticking to this plan by ...

The date of my next plan review will be ...

For some people, the plan can be activated immediately, either because there isn't much more practical planning involved or because they're less inclined to make excuses and delay starting. Regardless of what camp you're in, the next two chapters will look at ways to challenge any reasons you may have to delay your plan and to help you activate and sustain new, unfamiliar behaviours.

———

CHAPTER 17
NO MORE EXCUSES

——

Initially, it's important to put as many controllable things as possible into place that will increase the likelihood of you sustaining your plans. These can be anything from making sure any shopping you need has been done, to informing anyone else who will be affected by your plan, to setting reminders on your phone or taking photos of your maps so you can access them quickly. When working with clients, this can be a bit tricky sometimes, because on one hand I want them to invest time planning properly, while on the other I know that this window of time while they 'plan for their plan' can become an excuse to delay the start of their changes.

To decrease the likelihood of falling into a 'complacency trap', it's safest to assume that the possibility of relapse will be there for a long time. So you may always feel you need to go into certain situations having considered many different outcomes and decided how best to deal with them. Please be reassured, however, that extremely high levels of organisation and pre-emption are only required at the beginning of your change process. You will keep tweaking your plan until it is right for you, and then it will be a case of maintaining the new status quo, much of which will become second nature.
As you start to surprise yourself and change what becomes your 'norm', you will require less general and contingency planning to stay on track because:

- You'll have 'time under your belt' that you'll want to protect
- You'll be feeling accomplished and capable, which is something you'll want more of
- Other parts of your life that you hadn't considered before will have improved, either as a direct result of changing a specific practical habit or because of your increased confidence and the new choices you are making as a result
- You'll have overcome some high-risk situations that you probably doubted were possible, so you will feel more resilient when even triggers you hadn't considered catch you out
- You'll have naturally got into a routine that fits into your life more organically
- You'll be able to quickly recall your reasons to change and 'cut to the end' with your internal negotiations
- You'll have a new set of automatic behaviours (this time ones you've chosen)
- You'll have higher self-esteem and believe in your worthiness to achieve your long-term goals
- You will be more aware of self-sabotaging thoughts and less likely to believe them
- As you allow yourself to become kinder in the way you speak to yourself, there will be less to push out and avoid in the way of bullying, self-sabotaging thoughts
- You won't want to prove others right if they assume you won't keep your new habits up (although this isn't one that we are proud of admitting, it's real and in the short term it can really work to help us push through. In the long term, of course, the only doubter we should be concerned with proving wrong is ourselves)

I'd like to share a couple of common themes that run through conversations I have with my clients, either right before they start making changes or during the early stages of change, before they've reached the maintenance stage:

Overcoming Resentment and Self-pity

Whether it's the prospect of having to take action or finding it really difficult to stay on track for a few days in a row, as things start to get more challenging, a 'why me?' attitude can begin to creep in. Pre-empting this kind of thinking and deciding you won't allow it to derail your plans ahead of time can make all the difference.

Sometimes we feel sorry for ourselves because we find some things difficult that other people don't and therefore they don't need to have 'plans' at all. We may start to feel jealous of those who don't face the same the challenges as us and think we have a harder time of it than other people. This may well be true, but ruminating on it doesn't get us to where we want to be. Often it moves us further away.

I worked with a client once whose mother had introduced her to smoking heroin at a young age. By the time she was a teenager, she was a physically dependent injector of the drug and committing crimes to fund her habit as well as that of her mother (and her mother's partner). However, with the support of housing, probation services and substitute methadone prescriptions, she was able to turn her life around. During our first conversations, she was very resentful towards her mother, but over time this became closer to pity for the traumatic upbringing her mother had had. Whenever I start down the line of 'why me?' thinking, I always remember something this client said, which was not just kind but also extremely empowering: 'It's not my fault that it happened, but it's my responsibility to deal with it.'

Once they've explored their core beliefs, sometimes clients start to become resentful towards those who gave them these messages in the first place. This quote is also useful in these cases.

Another type of resentment can be towards me and the process. Sometimes clients aren't very happy to have to become more aware of their excuses to go off track. Once they've written them down and heard them out loud, it becomes more difficult for them to justify allowing themselves to be thrown off course, especially when these excuses are particularly absurd. As one of my clients put it, I took away her 'f*ck it' button. A commitment to becoming more self-aware and making choices on purpose can sometimes involve coming to terms with saying goodbye to this button. Life becomes less about 'getting out of it' and more about 'getting into it'.

When it comes to resentment and self-pitying feelings, some people never experience them at all. Sometimes they may experience a combination of many at once that come out of the blue. You may go weeks without having a single resentful or self-pitying thought, and then they hit you out of nowhere and you can't shake them for a while. As ever, when committing to becoming more self-aware, forewarned is forearmed. It's ultimately your choice whether you let these potentially sabotaging feelings turn into a definitely sabotaging action. One client recently told me that when she starts feeling resentful about having to have a plan in place for her drinking, she reminds herself that it's either sticking to a plan or sobriety for life. And since she wants to carry on drinking but never learned how to drink moderately, a strict plan was the best bet for her, whichever way she looked at it.

There are still rare occasions (usually if I'm particularly upset about something) when I want nothing more than to close the curtains and 'indulge myself' by bingeing on unhealthy foods and just 'escape' for a bit. But I know all too well where that ends up. I know that, rationally speaking, me abusing myself (whatever my personal definition of that is) will not change the situation that's upsetting me. Sometimes I look back at some of the excuses I made to myself that threw me off track and how creative my caveats were, and frankly I'm shocked that as an intelligent person I convinced myself that they were compelling arguments. In the early stages of change, when I still allowed one of these bogus arguments to 'work', I would write it down and determine that, at the very least, this would be the last time I let that particular one throw me off track. (That's not me giving you 'permission' to use every excuse you can think of one last time, by the way. Remember you don't need my permission, you're engaging in a voluntary process to make life more enjoyable for yourself in the long term.)

Sometimes clients become angry with themselves for having let things get to this stage. They begin thinking that if they'd started earlier, it wouldn't be so difficult for them to make changes. Or they think, 'If I started a year ago, by now I'd already be . . . .' The maps that capture negative aspects and impacts of their patterns make them realise that things are 'worse' than they initially thought. Instead of feeling proud to have faced things and acknowledged they need to make changes, they start feeling disappointed with themselves.

With regards to wishing you'd started earlier – sorry to be frank, but you didn't. Yes, it may be harder to change now than it would have been a year ago, but by the same logic it'll be harder still a year from now. The target dates you've written on your 'Life if I Do / Don't Make Changes' maps and your plan review will come around whether you change or not. Many clients have told me that they feel things are only ever getting better or worse when it comes to their habits, as opposed to staying the same for any sustained period. If this is the case, it may be useful to simply remember that the time will pass at the same rate whether you start now or not.

One of my former clients came up with a trick that she found really helpful. She had a five-spliff-per-day cannabis habit. She would often manage to stop altogether for a couple of weeks at a time, before lapsing back into her norm. She realised that on occasions when she wasn't feeling very resilient, she would find herself thinking, 'I've barely achieved anything here, not smoking for two weeks is hardly life-changing.' This would make her feel demoralised and as if her accomplishment wasn't significant, which would in turn contribute to justifying a lapse. (Even though when she was feeling resilient, she knew that after more than ten years of smoking every day, this was a huge achievement for her and worth acknowledging as one of the hardest things she'd ever done.) Once she had identified this as a trigger, she would tell herself to pretend she had actually stopped a year ago, which enabled her to embody the accomplished and determined attitude of someone who had a lot of time under their belt to protect.

Get Wise to Your Delaying Tactics

'Early days means I can just start again' thinking is very common. For example, imagine it's your plan activation day and it involves starting some kind of routine at home after work. Perhaps you've planned your evening meticulously. Everything you need is in place and you've created the conditions that give you the best possible chance of waking up to start Day Two feeling proud, accomplished and well on your way. You have every intention to stay on track all day and then, half an hour before you leave work, a colleague says she's had a difficult day. If this had happened a week earlier, you'd have offered to grab dinner with her, or stayed behind without thinking twice. Now you need to think about how to deal with this.

We all have priorities, and of course there will be occasions when someone you care about needs your help and this will become more immediately important to you than your habit change plan (although even here there are exceptions). However, it is important to keep in mind at this point that, especially in the early stages, you will often be in a state of swimming against a very heavy current and therefore waiting for any excuse you can pounce on to delay starting. You may even need to remind yourself that you're making the change in the first place (although if you've gone through all the maps in *The Kindness Method* up to this point, that's very unlikely to be the case!). Remember, your body and mind are used to things being one way and now you're trying to change that.

At the beginning, no matter how resilient you feel or how foolproof your plan seems, expect your motivation to waver from minute to minute. Bear in mind that even with this level of practical and emotional preparation, it's impossible to pre-empt how or when every possible triggering situation will present itself.

'No More Excuses' Map Guidance

With this in mind, we will now consider some of the excuses and delay tactics that may threaten your motivation. Based on experience, I would like you think about your common excuses and justifications for not starting, completing or sustaining a plan. First, write 'No More Excuses' in the centre of the map with a bubble around it. Then, note down your responses to the following cues, drawing a bubble around each entry as you go. See the example map at the end of the chapter.

Excuses and delaying tactics you've used in the past and don't want to use again
Excuses and delaying tactics you're already thinking of for this plan
Excuses you're likely to make in a few weeks to lapse from your plan

You may find it useful to use these sentence cues:

'Now isn't the right time because ...'
'It's not actually that important to change yet because ...'
'... is an exception because ...'
'... makes it impossible for me to change right now'
'Now I think about it, I was being unrealistic to think this plan would work because ...'

When you've finished, look through the excuses on your map and decide how you feel about them. Only you know if they look like convincing reasons when they're written down. If you believe that some of them are legitimate, of course that's absolutely fine. But I imagine that at least some of them are not worthy of being the reason you'd delayed the process of achieving your long-term goals.

Daily Kindness Check-ins

I see the process of building daily resilience against the temptation to go off track with plans of change as being like a cup that I'm always looking for opportunities to fill by making kind choices that make me feel good. For example:

- If the sun is unexpectedly shining and I have the time, I'll get off the tube a couple of stops early and walk the rest of the way through a park or along the canal
- If I've had a day of reading a lot of sad news, I'll make time to call a friend who I know I'm always able to have a laugh with
- If I see that a supermarket has reduced the price of flowers (and I can afford it), I buy myself some
- If I'm walking down the street and a car is waiting at traffic lights and blasting out a song I like, I might walk a little bit more slowly so I can listen to it

Sometimes the decisions are as tiny as staying in the shower for one minute longer than I need to, just to enjoy the feeling of standing under hot water.

I am always monitoring how full my cup feels, and when it's really low I have a few ideal go-tos and contingency go-tos that fill my cup quickly. An ideal go-to for me could be a solo visit to a karaoke booth. However, if it's raining, or I'm low on money or I just want to be indoors by myself, this may not be the best option at that time. So my contingency cup-filling plan tends to be things like looking at my 'Ways I'm Happy to Be' and 'What I'm Proud of' maps, turning off my phone, watching a film from childhood that I find comforting, lighting candles at home, calling a particularly supportive friend or just getting into bed really early and reading until I fall asleep. Some of my clients who have pets find that spending time with them can really help too.

It's also important to treat this process of being kind to ourselves as a serious and discerning one, one that's worth honouring. When I jump off the tube to enjoy the sunshine for those ten minutes, my phone is switched to 'do not disturb'. If I decide I could do with a positive conversation with a friend and they're not available, I find something else to do that will meet that need. I don't call a friend who I know will want to talk about how much she hates her job instead. Even as I write this, I hear myself thinking, 'That's selfish, you should always be there for people.' Those working in the helping professions will be familiar with the concept of 'burnout'. Urgent situations are an exception, of course, but in general I've learned I'm a much more generous and compassionate friend and family member when I'm first being generous and compassionate towards myself.

These little things don't only make us feel good and therefore strengthen our resolve, but deciding to do them reinforces the message that giving ourselves enjoyable experiences in our life is important and deserved. This, as we know, is the kind of thinking that helps us remember we're worthy of achieving our long-term goals.

Manage Your Expectations

Expect it to be hard. You knew it would be a struggle to change and you've voluntarily decided to do it anyway. This is an investment in your personal development which will pay out in all areas of life and help you achieve any goal you set yourself in the long term. Consider what your response would be if, at the beginning of this process, I asked you how difficult it would be to make changes that really last. How many minutes, hours, days of difficulty, discomfort and challenge would you expect to have to go through in the first month or two? These periods may be more difficult than you could ever imagine at times. But it can be very powerful and effective to expect these difficulties and, whenever possible, take the element of surprise out of the equation when they arise. A few of my clients will guess, say, ten days out of thirty will be really challenging. Then, when the fourth difficult day comes about, their resolve is strengthened by remembering that this was always inevitable and in fact they should expect another six!

Embody Not Just Who You Want to Be, But Who You Already Are

Sometimes we become so used to creating caveats and exceptions when it comes to our strengths and achievements that we don't act like they're true, even when they absolutely are. Some people find it hard to accept compliments without listing reasons why they aren't really deserved.

Look at your 'What I'm Proud of' map. If I'd told you when you were much younger that you'd have achieved those things, how would you imagine you'd be engaging with the world? Would you have a more grateful attitude, would you stand taller? Activating our plans is about embodying all the behaviours we assume that someone who had achieved what we've done and who possessed our strengths would express.

Something which really helped me to remember this was creating a poster that I have framed in my bedroom. It takes thirty seconds to read through in the morning. (I also have a photo of it on my phone and refer to it now and then.) Admittedly, I initially thought it was a bit silly but when I shared this suggestion with clients, many of them did the same thing and found it very useful. I've also started making these as gifts for friends who are suffering with 'imposter syndrome'. If you think this optional additional tool would be useful for you, it's very simple to put together.

To create the poster, take a collection of qualities from your 'Ways I'm Happy to Be' and 'What I'm Proud of' maps. Choose the ones that you're most proud of and genuinely believe to be unquestionably true. Then insert them into a template to print, like the one opposite:

HANNAH IS ...
Kind
Generous
Hardworking
Patient
Deserving of success
Fun
Accomplished
A good partner
Witty
Independent
Intelligent
Worthy of love
Unique
Friendly
Strong
WITH EVERY CHOICE YOU MAKE TODAY,
BEHAVE LIKE THESE THINGS ARE TRUE
BECAUSE THEY ARE

This tool can help remind you that addressing your chosen unwanted behaviour is just one small part of how you are going to change the way you engage with the world.

———

'No More Excuses' Map: Example

This map is a sample for guidance purposes only.

Make yours personal to you, in your own handwriting.

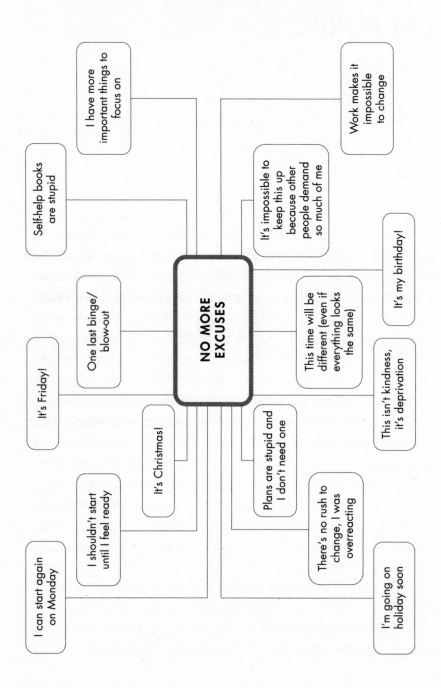

CHAPTER 18

TESTING MYSELF ON PURPOSE

——

As you start making changes, you will find yourself feeling more resilient and more easily able to overcome lots of predictable and unpredictable situations that will test your ability to stay on track. You will be tested in circumstances under which you've found it difficult or impossible to demonstrate your new habits in the past. With each of these challenges you notice yourself overcoming, add a new entry to your 'What I'm Proud of' map as quickly as possible. By seeing the task of populating the maps as a goal in itself, you will start to notice things you previously didn't give yourself credit for, or compliments and positive feedback you would otherwise have just forgotten.

Again, at first, before your new habits have started to really feel like your new norm, it can be useful to minimise the likelihood of lapse by avoiding high-risk situations (that you can control) as far as possible. However, adopting *The Kindness Method* involves doing everything you can to feel empowered and to face fears head-on, with resilience and courage. It's about realising that every time you face a high-risk situation and don't let that become a time to lapse, you are showing how much control you have over the choices you make for yourself. It's about changing those assumptions that begin with: 'I'm just the kind of person who can't . . .' or 'People like me will never be able to . . .'

We have already talked about anticipating and preparing for high-risk situations, but of course there will be times when we are tested out of nowhere. I believe that the best chance we have of dealing with these situations we can't imagine yet is to intentionally put ourselves in front of the ones we already know will challenge us, on purpose and on our own terms. In this way, we view the high-risk situations we can pre-empt as opportunities to show what we are capable of. This in turn puts us in a more resilient default position when faced with triggers that come out of the blue.

However, please bear in mind that trying this too early on is potentially a very dangerous game to play. When I am working one-to-one with a client, I am naturally able to assess whether I think it's time for them to start this exercise, based on their progress and a number of other factors. Sometimes clients have thought that they are ready to start testing themselves and I've suggested they wait a bit longer; perhaps reminding them that it wasn't very long ago they came very close to falling off track. In this case only you can decide when it feels right to start trying this exercise, but please be honest with yourself and remember that you're better off doing it in two months' time rather than bringing about a relapse that lasts for two months.

Even if you are quite far into your change process and doing so well that you can't even imagine the life you had before, the first few times you should still only try out this exercise when you are feeling at your most resilient. And always keep reassessing whether you are comfortable with the situation as the time to face it comes closer.

As is the case with a lot of things that scare us, overcoming our fear of being exposed to these threatening situations involves facing them head-on and expecting them to be difficult. Even if it's not difficult the first four times, you recognise that it's still possible for it to be difficult the fifth. And once you have overcome a high-risk situation, remember that you are potentially immediately presented with another one: complacency.

'Testing Myself on Purpose' Map

This map is a collection of specific scenarios you think are likely to test your resolve to stay on track with your current plan. Some of the entries on this map will include things you've written on your 'What Will Test Me?' map. The idea of this map is to tick off having overcome each one of these as many times as you need to in order to feel you're not vulnerable in this scenario.

'Testing Myself on Purpose' Map Guidance Part 1

To complete this map, first write 'Testing Myself on Purpose' in the middle of a blank page, drawing a bubble around it. Then write down your answers to the questions below. See the example map at the end of the chapter.

These, and any others you can think of, will form the collection of situations and scenarios that you will need to overcome a considerable number of times before you can genuinely believe you've changed for good.

What circumstances will test my motivation the most?
What difficult situations would I be proud to face head-on
     and overcome, without reverting back to the behaviour I'm trying
     to change?
What specific hurdles have I never quite seemed to jump over when
     it came to making changes last?
What events/situations do I already know are coming up, that are
     likely to make me want to give up/revert to my unwanted habits?

'Testing Myself on Purpose' Map Guidance Part 2

When you have completed your map for now, and you have a list of high-risk situations you expect to face, think about the number of times you think you'd have to overcome each one under as many different circumstances as you can, before you'd be confident that it's no longer a high-risk situation for you. Create this number of tick boxes next to each situation. You can, of course, increase this number if you get close to the goal but recognise that you still need many more successful instances under your belt before it stops feeling like a serious challenge. The speed at which you work through these is up to you. Some opportunities to tick them off may well catch you by surprise. When they do, you can observe whether there is still a strong 'pull' back to your old habits, especially in the moments when you're least prepared for a test.

When you have overcome a high-risk situation more than enough times for it not to cause your motivation to waver at all, you can put a big satisfying cross through the whole section.

When Is a Habit Changed for Good?

This will differ from person to person and from habit to habit. It's safe to say that if, when you explored the ways that the habit was serving you, you realised there were barely any, and even those you could think of were not particularly important for you, then there will be few (if any) forces pulling you back to old ways, other than just plain old what you've been used to.

I often hear those with experience of drug addiction debating whether they should consider themselves as always being 'in recovery', or whether they should consider themselves 'recovered'. There is sound reasoning for both approaches, and I have seen them work equally well. *The Kindness Method* is more aligned with the latter type of thinking, and presumes that although we should remain wary and aware of how ingrained some of our habits were, life is punctuated with the successful completion of many little 'recovery plans', with their own associated challenges that we face head-on enough times until they are not challenging any more.

Mark Your Milestones and Celebrate

We so often celebrate and reward ourselves by 'letting ourselves off the hook' because we've done so well. In this process there is no hook. One of the most important parts of sustaining long-term change is to see it as part of a bigger process of continually moving forward towards a life you enjoy, on purpose. It is amazing how quickly some changes become our new norm and how quickly we can forget the grip some of them had on us. For this reason, it's important to keep recording all of our new achievements and developments on our maps, as well as finding new ways to celebrate them.

So many people only reward themselves for managing not to do something by doing the thing they've managed not to do! This not only limits the ways we can enjoy celebrating but also reduces an exciting plan of change to a little game we play with ourselves where we're rewarding ourselves for managing not to 'be bad' by allowing ourselves to do the 'bad' thing for a bit.

———

'Testing Myself on Purpose' Map: Example

This map is a sample for guidance purposes only.

Make yours personal to you, in your own handwriting.

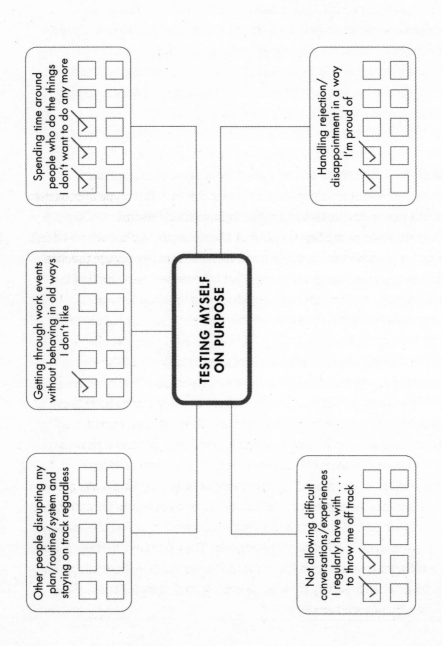

CHAPTER 19
ALCOHOL

A lot of the work I do is with clients who want to change their behaviours around alcohol, and this section includes some approaches and tips that those particular clients have found useful.

This is one of the few sections of *The Kindness Method* where I don't draw from addiction treatment but instead from my private practice in behavioural-change coaching. That is because when working in addictions, I had targets to meet which were mainly focused on abstinence; not least because the impact drinking was having on a client's day-to-day life had usually become extremely problematic, often debilitating and, in many cases, life-threatening. The vast majority of my current clients, however, have had a few concerning incidents and feel that elements of their drinking habits have become problematic enough to address. As such, they want an opportunity to pause to think about why they drink, what they drink and how they can ensure that alcohol is serving them as a truly recreational substance, rather than it being imperative that they stop it altogether.

Clients often feel that their lifestyles have outgrown their drinking habits while their tolerance has increased, and therefore the amount they spend on alcohol has also gone up. They tend not to like the fact that they associate so many common experiences with drinking, and would like to diversify their go-to coping strategies for stress relief, boredom or social anxiety.

Controlled Experiments

In keeping with the idea of treating habit change firstly as a process of self-enquiry, it's useful, when you start thinking about something like changing how you drink, to keep variables to a minimum. The best way I've found to do this is to stick to one type of drink to begin with. Aside from the fact that many of my clients report feeling different effects from different types of alcohol, if we want to create a new 'way' of drinking, we need first to know how our bodies are responding to specific amounts of alcohol under different circumstances. For example, it can be useful to notice how quickly you drink some drinks compared to others, or which ones you seem to associate with low mood. Sometimes something as simple as having a rule never to drink on an empty stomach can change the landscape of the next day entirely.

'Coming Up'

Very often clients report drinking so quickly that they 'reach a point of no return' too early on in an evening, and find themselves more drunk than they'd like to – or intended to – be. To generalise, they tend to discover through our conversations that this is because they have carried over adolescent drinking styles into adulthood. For example, they're drinking quickly, back to back, and not leaving time for the drug to set in. It's as though having a good time is associated with constantly continuing to consume alcohol as opposed to enjoying the effects of it.

The clients for whom this thinking has been something of a revelation are often those who have in the past used drugs like ecstasy, where they would consume a dose of something and wait to see what effect it had on their body before consuming any more. Even in the case of coffee, it's reasonable to refuse a second because we're waiting for it to 'hit' us and we don't want to accidentally go all jittery.

I've often observed that this is not how some people behave with alcohol (or, incidentally, with sugar). Through conversations with clients, I'm starting to wonder if this is at least partly because they are among the first very effective, very available drugs we're exposed to. Many clients report that their first opportunities to use alcohol involved being encouraged by peers to drink as much as possible, in as short a time as possible, before someone gets picked up by a parent or gets caught. You may be thinking it's juvenile for adults to be discussing these issues in a session, but I have worked with a number of very emotionally intelligent, professionally accomplished, highly capable clients in their forties who have only discovered through our work that they haven't stopped to rethink the way they drink since they were seventeen years old.

Finding the Sweet Spot

In order to get the most out of any drug, would it not make sense, once the desired effect has been achieved, to stay there as long as possible? Rather than to apply the logic that if something is good, more of it would be more good, it can help to remember that with some drugs there can in fact be diminishing rewards with each additional dose we take. In the case of alcohol, it can be useful instead to identify your sweet spot and just top up when you think you need it to feel the required effects. For many of my clients this has been a helpful way to decrease the amount they drink, because they realise that truly enjoying the effects they desire from alcohol – and sustaining that feeling for as long as possible – requires them to drink much less and more slowly.

Very often, when clients report feeling regretful about how much they drank the night before, I ask them to tell me what they remember as being the part of the evening when they felt like alcohol was doing the best job. The period when it made them feel relaxed, their inhibitions lowered, their (perceived) confidence higher, but when they also still felt in control and in a positive mood. Almost without exception, clients report this being very early on in the evening. And yet, they continued to drink past this 'sweet spot'.

This was another area where I noticed parallels with attempting to moderate my eating. Both food and alcohol can absolutely be enjoyable and of course we can associate them with positive experiences. The kindness stops when we don't appreciate that often with each decision of consuming an additional slice of cake or glass of wine, the returns are diminishing for us overall.

To identify your 'alcohol sweet spot' try this exercise. Think back to the last time(s) you remember drinking in a way you were happy with – not just while you were drinking but also the day after. Consider these questions:

At what point in the drinking experience was I enjoying the alcohol most?
How much had I had to drink?
What was I drinking?
What had I eaten before?
What kind of day was I having/how was I feeling when I started drinking?
Was I using alcohol to 'get out of it' or get into it?

What Kind of Drinker/Eater/(Insert Behaviour of Your Choice) Do You Want to Be?

Many of my clients have found that as they've got older, their recovery time for hangovers has increased. Sometimes, simultaneously their interest in drinking has increased. For instance, a couple of my clients are very interested in wine, and for them the financial aspect of their habit is not a concern. The way they have decreased how much they drink and their approach to drinking is to reframe it as a pleasure as opposed to an escape, and to drink better wine but less of it – and to really enjoy it.

Most clients tell me that, regardless of tolerance, finances or the severity and duration of hangovers, they don't want to drink in the same way in their thirties as they did in their twenties, or in their forties as they did in their thirties. Often they have used illegal drugs in the past, which never became problematic for various reasons, but largely because they always knew that buying them and the relationships that came with them would just naturally cease to fit in with their lifestyles as they got older. However, as alcohol is both legal and associated with everything from football games to Fridays to funerals, that natural shift sometimes doesn't take place without us deciding that it needs to.

It can be useful to think about ways you can reframe how you view drinking so that it feels right for the lifestyle you want to maintain at any given life stage. One client I recently worked with started drinking alcohol differently after a trip to Italy, where he observed how Italians were consuming the drug. He enjoyed adopting the slower pace of drinking and admired the way the substance was being handled as an 'optimisation tool', something to complement an already enjoyable experience such as a dinner or socialising in a context that was already accommodating and comfortable. Now when he's tempted to drink to excess or veer off the plans he has set himself (which now also include coffee and food), he has a rule that he asks himself: ' What would an Italian do?'

––––––

CHAPTER 20
FALLING OFF THE WAGON...
(AND GETTING ON AGAIN)
___

Substance-misuse practitioners often find themselves saying two things that seem conflicting but are simultaneously correct:
- A lapse is an important learning opportunity!
- (but) Not lapsing *at all* is what you're aiming for!

It is important to remember that if you do lapse you can absolutely get back on track immediately and you needn't allow it to become a relapse. However, it's also important to remember that most people *will* lapse and that the lapse itself might make it more challenging to keep your conversations with yourself helpful and kind, at least in the short term, before you're back on track again.

I once worked with a twenty-two-year-old female client who had been in abstinent recovery from alcohol for seven months. She described feeling unexpectedly 'triggered' and that she couldn't stop thinking about using, because one of her close friends in the recovery community had lapsed. Although they had got back on track really quickly, she described the sadness she felt for her friend, as well as the fear and shock of realising how easily a lapse can happen. She was experiencing a lot of frightened 'it could have just as easily been me' thinking. But she admitted to me the thing that was triggering her the most about her friend's lapse was the fact she'd managed 'to get away with it'. My client had witnessed someone coming through seemingly unharmed and still surrounded by support, despite dipping a toe back into a behaviour she had been holding at bay for months, after presuming a lapse would be catastrophic. Seeing first hand that perhaps that might not be the case was tempting her to lapse herself, and she had started having more 'using thoughts' and 'using dreams'.

Be Honest About Feeling Tempted

I'd often heard addiction-treatment professionals say that even if their clients are feeling more tempted to use than they have been in a long time, it's an excellent sign if they're openly talking about it. I've often seen in groups when someone shares how tempted they have been to use, how many people relate to that. Often, just the acknowledgement of it in itself is enough to stop the lapse from happening.

Naturally, how difficult it is to get back on track will depend on what you have set out to address and what you have decided to define as a relapse. The impact that a lapse has on someone's life is unique. One trigger for a lapse turning into a relapse can be seeing how easily you were able to revert to old ways. It can be really demoralising to realise how normal it can still feel to engage in habits you've long since changed. At those times, it can be useful to remember that the comfortable, familiar way had its benefits, as we have acknowledged. It wasn't all negative; you knew that early on.

'Relapse Reminder Snapshot' Map

Imagine you are feeling unexpectedly and strongly drawn back to old ways. You urgently glance at a map you've already created to help you push through these moments and remember in one glance why you should carry on, no matter how hard it gets in that moment. That's your 'Relapse Reminder Snapshot' Map you will create now. First, write 'Relapse Reminder Snapshot' in the middle of a blank page, with a bubble drawn around it. Then, note down your responses to the questions below, drawing a bubble around each entry. Naturally, feel free to note down any quick reminders you think would be useful to glance at in an emergency situation! See the example map at the end of the chapter.

> What things can I say to myself as a quick reminder of how important it is for me to stay on track?
> Who might be able to help me? How? What's their number?
> What could I easily do or focus on instead of giving in to cravings/urges?

Creating Urgency to Get Back on Track

If you've lapsed, and in response you find yourself wanting to get back on track immediately, it can be useful to create short-term variations of the 'Life if I Don't Make Changes' and the 'Life if I Do Make Changes' maps. For example, 'What will I be saying to myself in three days if I'm not back on track?' versus 'What will I be saying to myself in three days if I am back on track?'

Specify what your 'get back on track' plan needs to involve and what it needs to avoid. If you had previously planned to be in an avoidable risky situation, make a concerted effort not to go there in the short term. This is because you are at risk of being demoralised by the disappointment of going off track and it will make you more vulnerable to self-sabotaging behaviours and unhelpful thoughts like, 'I've ruined all that time I had under my belt . . .'

Knowing that a lapse doesn't need to become a relapse is a lesson that can be applied to achieving moderation in a range of life areas. The more we practise challenging our excuses, the less they will pop up in the first place. There are no foods that I have resolved to never eat again, but there are certainly some that I generally consider 'lapse' foods. That doesn't mean I avoid them, it just means that I'm aware they may trigger old 'all or nothing' thinking patterns about food. If I choose to act on them I consider it a harmless, conscious blip and move on as quickly as possible. Negotiations are very uncommon for me these days because I seem to just cut to the end and apply what I know about lapse management: the more time I waste beating myself up, the further I get from where I want to be, in every possible way.

Recognise the Warning Signs

Often when it feels like a lapse has occurred almost out of nowhere, if we really reflect back it becomes clear that we'd missed some early-warning signs that trouble was brewing. This is an example of an early-warnings checklist completed by someone in recovery from alcohol abuse.

- Attending meetings less regularly or missing them completely
- Not doing enough planning around how I will get to meetings
- Losing touch with important members of my recovery support network
- Neglecting my personal hygiene
- Not making time for mindful practice
- Not taking pride in my appearance and my surroundings
- Starting to get into old negative patterns of thinking about myself and others
- Making contact with acquaintances from the past who are still using
- Making less of an effort to avoid or plan for my high-risk situations
- Not nurturing relationships with my family and friends
- Isolating myself and not calling on my supporter in times of need
- Adopting other unhealthy/unwanted habits
- Failing to notice and acknowledge increasing feelings of resentment, anger and frustration
- Neglecting my physical health
- Not getting enough fresh air
- Neglecting my finances and getting myself into debt
- Missing medical appointments or important meetings
- Becoming sleep-deprived or not ensuring I get quality rest

It may be worth creating your own list of subtle early-warning signs to help you become more aware of them creeping up in different combinations and to varying degrees. As one of my clients recently put it when describing relapses that initially appeared to come from nowhere, 'Looking back, you always realise it was the ants that carried you away, not the elephant.'

Whenever You're Ready

If you find yourself in a sustained relapse with a particular habit, you can start working through the relevant maps again whenever you're ready. The beauty of this process is that things like 'not succeeding' and 'starting again' only apply to each isolated change plan itself. The majority of the groundwork required to 'start again' on an even better footing has, in fact, already been done. A lot of it has been captured in black and white. The rest of it you're already doing every day by consciously choosing to become more and more aware of your own patterns. There's a non-judgemental framework waiting patiently for whenever you feel ready again. Hopefully by now you're already treating yourself with more kindness across all areas of your life, regardless of what stage you're at with any specific plan at any given time.

———

CHAPTER 21
CRUISE CONTROL
____

Whether it's compulsively reaching for a drink or compulsively checking your phone, I hope at the very least to have encouraged you to shift more focus to the 'compulsively' part.

Of course, it's much easier said than done, and it will always be difficult for us to change our ingrained habits. Although exercises like the ones in this book are designed to help you start to become more aware of your thoughts and behaviours in general, what you do with those observations will always be up to you. A conscious and often very difficult decision has to be made to tune in with curiosity to our thoughts and feelings when we want nothing more than to hastily act on our triggers. It's your finger on the 'f*ck it' button, and early on in any change process, you can expect to feel like you're constantly hovering above it.

The good news is that you'll be less tempted to press it over time, as you'll gradually feel you have less to avoid and distract yourself from. You will be more comfortable sitting in discomfort and just observing it. And you'll have proven to yourself over and over again that no amount of annoying colleagues or bad weather or mind-numbing boredom can actually make you act unkindly towards yourself. Even in those moments when the internal messages are familiarly unkind and uncomfortably convincing, YOU decide whether to treat them as cruel commands or curious observations. When it comes to your unwanted habits, you will have disassociated the word kindness with things like 'immediate relief' and 'letting yourself off the hook'. Instead, you will now associate kindness with acting and speaking to yourself in a manner that moves you most quickly towards the most exciting and enjoyable life you can imagine.

While writing this book, the changes that have taken place in my own life have admittedly tested my ability to keep unwanted old habits at bay. Although I am proud not to have acted on them in ways I'm not happy with, at points it's felt like I was being constantly triggered in ways I had never considered and could never have begun to plan for. After a long stretch of steady cruising with my new, kinder habits and a practically permanent feeling of resilience against my old ones, I was disappointed to realise recently that my ability to start telling myself unkind stories may always be there.

Luckily, I have also observed that a few things have remained changed for me in a very fundamental way for a while now, and seem to be continuously changing for the better. How often I indulge the unkind stories: rarely. How often I allow them to derail my plans: never.

Acknowledgements

No one has shaped my therapeutic approach and professional style as much as Ray Jenkins. He has been my trainer, boss, colleague, mentor, champion and friend, and I could never repay him for the opportunities he has given me.

It's thanks to Marisa Bate's series of brave and relatable articles that I was approached to write *The Kindness Method* by my (now) agent, Sarah Williams who has guided me through every step of this process. It's also thanks to Sarah that I have been able to work with Carole Tonkinson and her incredibly supportive team at Bluebird.

Friends and family have helped me in a number of different ways, not least during the months when I was writing alone in my flat. They proofread, tried out maps, and provided useful feedback that really shaped the book. I was also the recipient of many reassuring late-night calls, sage professional advice, much-needed pep talks and many, many celebrations. Thank you Saven Chadha, Joel Champion, Aida Faryar, Rachel Firth, Hannah Firth, Sara Firth, Alba Gutierrez, Grace Gutierrez, Chris Gutierrez, Alborz Izadi, Paul Jagger, Miriam Kilpatrick, Diane Laidlaw, Will Lewis, Sarah Mitchell, Fipsi Seilern, James Severin, Tom Upchurch and Sam Welton.

My parents have also shown me an enormous amount of support, compassion and generosity, for which I am incredibly grateful.

Finally, thank you to those in long-term recovery, for teaching me so much about resilience, self-awareness and kindness.